General Knowledge
Knowledge
Olympiad

Class 10

General Knowledge Olympiad

Class 10

A must have book for all Olympiads & Talent Search Exams...

by
Vivek Sharma

BLoOM CAP
Bloom Cap Edu Ventures Pvt. Ltd.

Bloom Cap Edu Ventures Pvt. Ltd.

꣩ **Administrative & Production Office**

'Ramchhaya' 4577/15, Agarwal Road, Darya Ganj, New Delhi -110002
Tele: 011- 47630600, 43518550

꣩ **ISBN :** 978-93-25519-49-7

꣩ **PRICE :** ₹100.00

꣩ **PO No :** TXT-XX-XXXXXXX-X-XX

For further information about the books log on to
www.bloomcap.org

Follow us on   

Preface

"Future belongs to those Who prepares for it today"

School Olympiads are National & International level competitions conducted by different Government, Non-Government & Educational Organisations with the purpose of making the children ready to face competitive exams. The challenging Questions asked in Olympiads motivate them to learn more & more and bring out the best result with improved academic performance. The Awards & Scholarship offered by Olympiads motivate children to aspire & strive for doing better and emerge out to be the best.

GK Olympiads

GK is the knowledge of every aspect of the human life, which may or may not be the part of routine academic studies but very important for the overall personality development of the students. It is more or less connected with the attentiveness and awareness. There can be different domains of GK like; History, Geography, Polity, Culture, Discovery, Sports, Current Affairs etc.

GK Olympiads help students in understanding the importance of General Knowledge and updations about National & International Affairs in daily life.

'Bloom GK Olympiad Study Book Class 10' is a perfect resource to Study & Practice for Olympiad Exams and other National & State Level Talent Search Exams & Other Competitions.

Some Special Features of Bloom GK Olympiad Study Books are;

- Complete coverage of all the topics related to GK;. History, Geography, Environment, Polity, Science, Sports, etc.
- Chapterwise Exercises having different types of Objective Questions.
- Olympiad Pattern Practice Sets at the end.

This book is prepared by Expert Panel with the utmost care, still if you have any suggestions regarding its improvement then feel free to contact us at olympiads@bloomcap.org. We will try to inculcate your suggestions in the further editions.

Contents

Ancient History

1 Mark Questions

1. Which of these Indus Valley Civilisation sites does not lie in India?
   (a) Kalibangan   (b) Lothal
   (c) Rangpur   (d) Chanhudaro

2. Which of the following Indus cities was known for water management?
   (a) Lothal   (b) Mohenjo Daro
   (c) Dholavira   (d) Harappan

3. The Indus valley people did not produce which of these crops?
   (a) Rice   (b) Wheat
   (c) Barley   (d) Mustard

4. Which of the following sites is also known as 'Manchester of Indus Valley Civilisation'?
   (a) Lothal   (b) Kalibangan
   (c) Harappa   (d) Surkotada

5. In which veda, Varna system was discussed?
   (a) Rigveda   (b) Yajurveda
   (c) Samaveda   (d) Atharvaveda

6. Most of the hymns in the Rigveda are attributed to which of the following?
   (a) The God of Fire
   (b) The God of Rains
   (c) The God of Plants
   (d) The God of Farmers

7. King Ashoka is often referred by what name in his inscriptions?
   (a) Dharmadeva   (b) Chakravartin
   (c) Samarat   (d) Devanamapriya

8. Which great Buddhist Monk headed the third Buddhist Council held under Ashoka?
   (a) Nagarjuna
   (b) Ananda
   (c) Moggaliputta Tissa
   (d) Asanga

9. Ashokan inscriptions occupy a very significant place in the history of India. Which of these languages have not been used by Ashoka in his inscription?
   (a) Prakrit   (b) Aramaic
   (c) Magadhi   (d) Greek

10. Which of the following animals has never been used by Ashoka in his Pillar Capitals?
    (a) Elephant   (b) Lion
    (c) Bull   (d) Eagle

11. With which of the following educational centers, Chanakya was associated?
    (a) Taxila   (b) Nalanda
    (c) Vikramshila   (d) None of these

12. Who was called as 'Second Ashoka'?
(a) Kanishka
(b) Samudragupta
(c) Chandragupta
(d) Harshavardhana

13. The Gandhara art flourished under
....
(a) the Guptas   (b) the Mauryas
(c) the Kushans   (d) the Satvahanas

14. The great Chinese Scholar Fa-Hien visited India during the reign of which of the following Kings?
(a) Meghavarna   (b) Chandragupta II
(c) Ashoka   (d) Samudragupta

15. Who was the court poet of King Harshavardhana?
(a) Kalidasa   (b) Banabhatta
(c) Harisena   (d) Jayadeva

2 Marks Questions

16. Consider the following statements.

1. Copper was the first metal used by Vedic People.
2. The people of Vedic civilisation practiced agriculture and pastoralism.
3. The references to agriculture are mainly found in the Atharva Veda.

Which of the given statements is/are true?

Codes
(a) Only 1 and 2   (b) Only 2 and 3
(c) Only 1 and 3   (d) Only 2

17. Which of the following were main aims of the Dhamma of Ashoka?

1. To counter religious tension in the society.
2. To propagate the idea of Buddhism in his empire.
3. To encourage the attitude of social responsibility among people.

Which of the statements given above is/are true?

Codes
(a) Only 1   (b) Only 2
(c) Only 1 and 2   (d) All of these

18. Match the following.

List I (Harappan Site)		List II (Located at)
A.	Kalibangan	1. Haryana
B.	Banawali	2. Baluchistan
C.	Dholavira	3. Rajasthan
D.	Sutkagendor	4. Gujarat

Codes

	A	B	C	D		A	B	C	D
(a)	1	2	3	4	(b)	2	1	4	3
(c)	2	4	1	3	(d)	3	1	4	2

19. Match the following.

List I (Ancient Text)		List II (Written by)
A.	Rajataringini	1. Harshavardhan
B.	Abhigyanam Shakuntalam	2. Kalidasa
C.	Ratnavali	3. Kalhana
D.	Gitagovinda	4. Jayadeva

Codes

	A	B	C	D		A	B	C	D
(a)	3	2	1	4	(b)	2	3	1	4
(c)	3	1	2	4	(d)	4	2	3	1

Medieval History

1 Mark Questions

1. Which of these Pala rulers established a new University named Vikramshila?
   (a) King Gopala
   (b) King Dharampala
   (c) King Devpala
   (d) King Mahendrapala

2. Which among the following kings were the founder of Pala dynasty?
   (a) Dharampala
   (b) Rajyapala
   (c) Gopala
   (d) Govindapala

3. Name the Italian traveller, who visited the Vijanagar empire in AD 1420.
   (a) Nicolo de Conti
   (b) Abdur Rajjak
   (c) Marco Polo
   (d) Barbosa

4. In the Second Battle of Tarain, Prithviraj Chauhan was defeated by which of these Turkish invader?
   (a) Mahmud Ghaznavi
   (b) Ghiyas-ud-din Muhammad
   (c) Muizzudin Muhammad
   (d) Qutubuddin Aibak

5. Timur the Lame invaded India in 1398 that ended which of the following dynasties of the Delhi Sultanate?
   (a) Khilji Dynasty
   (b) Tughlaq Dynasty
   (c) Lodi Dynasty
   (d) Mamluk Dynasty

6. Who introduced the Ghazal style of singing in India?
   (a) Mirza Ghalib   (b) Abu Faiz
   (c) Amir Khusrau   (d) Gulbadan Begam

7. Abdur Razzak, the Persian traveller visited Vijayanagara during the reign of which of the following?
   (a) Deva Raya II
   (b) Deva Raya I
   (c) Krishna Deva Raya
   (d) Venkat I

8. Krishna Deva Raya, the great Vijayanagara king belonged to which of the following dynasty?
   (a) Saluva Dynasty
   (b) Tuluva Dynasty
   (c) Sangam Dynasty
   (d) None of the above

9. Which of the following describes Jizyahor Jizya correctly?
   (a) A tax imposed on temples for their protection by Muslim Rulers.
   (b) A tax imposed on Hindu priests by Muslim Rulers.
   (c) A tax imposed on non-muslim people by Muslim Rulers.
   (d) A tax imposed on the Hindu Zamindars by Muslim Rulers.

10. The Tomb of Salim Chishti was built by Akbar inside which of these monuments?
    (a) Red Fort, Delhi
    (b) Fatehpur Sikri, Agra
    (c) Humayun's Tomb, Delhi
    (d) Agra Fort, Agra

11. Akbar divided his empire into how many provinces?
    (a) Twelve   (b) Fifteen
    (c) Nine   (d) Nineteen

12. Which of these Mughal kings abolished the practise of forcible conversion of Prisoners of War?
    (a) Aurangzeb   (b) Shah Jahan
    (c) Akbar   (d) Humayun

13. Which among the following was not among the nine Jewels of Akbar?
    (a) Man Singh
    (b) Abdul Rahim Khan i Khana
    (c) Aziao Din
    (d) Dhanvantri

14. Which of the following courtiers of Akbar translated the Bible into Persian?
    (a) Raja Man Singh
    (b) Faizi
    (c) Raja Todar Mal
    (d) Abul Fazl

15. Which of the following introduced the Zabt System of revenue administration during the Mughal rule?
    (a) Sayyid Hussain Ali Khan
    (b) Raja Man Singh
    (c) Mullah do Pyaza
    (d) Raja Todarmal

16. Who among the following translated the Mahabharata into Persian during the period of Mughal rule?
    (a) Gharat Khan
    (b) Nizamuddin Ahmad
    (c) Abul Fazl
    (d) Abdul Qadir Badauni

2 Marks Questions

17. Consider the following statements.
    1. The city of Vijayanagar was situated on the banks of river Krishna.
    2. Krishnadeva Raya earned the title of Andhra Bhoja.
    3. The Vijayanagara Empire ended with the Battle of Tallikota.

    Which of the statements given above are true?

    Codes
    (a) Only 1 and 2   (b) Only 1 and 3
    (c) Only 2 and 3   (d) 1, 2 and 3

18. Consider the following statements.
    1. Shivaji was a member of Bhonsle Maratha clan.
    2. Due to his Guerilla warfare tactics, he was called Mountain Rat by Aurangzeb.

3. Ashtapradhan were appointed by Shivaji for efficient administration of state.

Which of the statements given above is/are true?

Codes

(a) Only 1   (b) Only 3

(c) 1, 2 and 3   (d) Only 1 and 3

19. Consider the following statements regarding 'Third Battle of Panipat'.

   1. It was fought between Mughals and Afghans.

   2. Ahmad Shah Durrani was the leader of Afghan Forces.

   3. Nawab of Awadh provided support to Afghans.

Which of the statements given above is/are true?

Codes

(a) Only 1   (b) Only 2

(c) Only 3   (d) Only 2 and 3

20. Match the following.

List I (Monument)		List II (Built by)	
A.	Alai Darwaza	1.	Alaudin Khilji
B.	Tughlaqabad Fort	2.	Shah Jahan
C.	Wazir Khan Mosque	3.	Ghazi Malik
D.	Rohtas Fort	4.	Sher Shah

Codes

	A	B	C	D
(a)	2	1	3	4
(b)	1	3	2	4
(c)	2	3	1	4
(d)	3	2	1	4

Chapter 03

Modern History

1 Mark Questions

1. Which of the following was the last to come to India as a trading company?
   (a) Danes
   (b) French
   (c) Danish
   (d) English

2. The First Factory of Portuguese East India Company was established at which place?
   (a) Kakinata
   (b) Bombay
   (c) Masulipatnam
   (d) Calicut

3. Which Mughal Emperor defeated the English East India Company in the one and only Anglo Mughal War?
   (a) Bahadur Shah Zafar
   (b) Aurangzeb
   (c) Farrukhsiyar
   (d) Akbar II

4. Which of the following battle was won by the British to get full control of Bengal, Bihar and Odisha?
   (a) Battle of Plassey
   (b) Battle of Wandiwash
   (c) Battle of Buxar
   (d) Battle of Ushant

5. Who became the Nawab of Bengal after the British killed Sirajuddaulah in the famous Battle of Plassey?
   (a) Mir Qasim   (b) Mir Madan
   (c) Rai Durlabh   (d) Mir Jafar

6. Which state was the first to accept the imposition of the Subsidiary Alliance of Lord Wellesley?
   (a) Bengal   (b) Awadh
   (c) Hyderabad   (d) Junagadh

7. Which of the following annexed Jhansi under the Doctrine of Lapse?
   (a) Lord Wellesley (b) Warren Hastings
   (c) Lord Dalhouise (d) Lord Cornwallis

8. Which of the following British Viceroys took the very first step in introducing local bodies (Panchayati Raj) in India?
   (a) Lord Lytton   (b) Lord Mayo
   (c) Lord Ripon   (d) Lord Dalhousie

9. The first telegraph line in India was started between which of the following places?
   (a) Bombay to Pune
   (b) Bombay to Thane
   (c) Sutanati to Govindpur
   (d) Calcutta to Diamond Harbour

10. Mahalwari System of revenue administration was introduced by which of the following?
(a) Thomas Munro
(b) Alexander Read
(c) Holt Mackanzie
(d) Lord Cornwallis

11. The system of civil services was introduced in India by which of the following?
(a) Lord Dalhouise
(b) Lord Cornwallis
(c) Lord Wellesley
(d) Lord Macaulay

12. Who was the Governor General of India during the revolt of 1857?
(a) Lord Lytton
(b) Lord Dufferin
(c) Lord Lansdowne
(d) Lord Canning

13. Mangal Pandey, one of the earliest freedom fighters belonged to which of the following British regiments?
(a) 72nd Bengal Native Infantry
(b) 3rd Bengal Native Cavalry
(c) 34th Bengal Native Infantry
(d) United Malwa Contingent Cavalry

14. Which among the following did not participate in the Great Revolt of 1857?
(a) Bakht Khan
(b) Rani Lakshmibai
(c) Tantia Tope
(d) Karam Shah

15. Which of the following freedom fighters was defeated by the British at Kanpur after which he escaped to Nepal?
(a) Rao Sahib
(b) Maulvi Ahmadullah
(c) Nana Sahib
(d) Tantia Tope

16. During the revolt of 1857, Rani Lakshmibai captured Gwalior from the British with the help of which among the following?
(a) Kunwar Singh
(b) Tantia Tope
(c) Nana Saheb
(d) Khan Bahadur Khan

17. The first Supreme Court of India was established under which Governor-General?
(a) Lord Wellesley   (b) Warren Hastings
(c) Lord Minto   (d) Lord Canning

18. Which of the following British Commanders suppressed the revolt of 1857 at Gwalior and Jhansi?
(a) General Hugh Rose
(b) William Taylor
(c) Colin Campbell
(d) John Nicolson

19. Which of the following social reformers established the Prarthana Samaj?
(a) Keshub Chandra Sen
(b) Dadoba Pandurang
(c) Ferozshah Mehta
(d) Swami Vivekananda

2 Marks Questions

20. Which of the following pairs (Administrators and their designations) is incorrectly matched?
(a) Robert Clive-First Governor of Bengal
(b) William Bentinck-First Governor General of India
(c) Lord Canning-First Viceroy of India
(d) Lord Mountbatten-Last Governor General of India

21. Which of the following statements is/are true?

1. The first railway line was laid during the period of Lord Dalhouise.
2. Lord Ripon was the Viceroy of India when Queen Victoria became the Empress of India.

Codes
(a) Only 1   (b) Only 2
(c) Both 1 and 2   (d) None of these

22. Which of the following statements is/are true?

1. After the Battle of Buxar, the British company acquired monopoly over Indian trade.
2. British company imposed heavy duties on export of cotton products from India.
3. British company exported raw materials from India to support industries of Britain.

Codes
(a) Only 1   (b) Only 3
(c) Both 1 and 3   (d) All of these

23. Match the following.

List I (Settlement)		List II (European Power)	
A.	Pondicherry	1.	French
B.	Goa	2.	Portuguese
C.	Transquebar	3.	Danes
D.	Masulipatnam	4.	Dutch

Codes

	A	B	C	D
(a)	1	2	3	4
(b)	2	3	4	1
(c)	1	2	4	3
(d)	3	4	1	2

Chapter 04

National Movement

1 Mark Questions

1. The East India Association was founded by Dadabhai Naoroji at which of these places?
   (a) New York
   (b) Brussels
   (c) London
   (d) Paris

2. Which of the following was not set up by Gandhiji in South Africa?
   (a) News paper Indian opinion
   (b) The Natal Indian Congress
   (c) The Phoenix Ashram
   (d) The Indian League

3. Who became the first President of the Bombay Presidency Association?
   (a) Badruddin Tyabji
   (b) Pherozeshah Mehta
   (c) Dadabhai Naoroji
   (d) Ananda Mohan Bose

4. Lokmanya Tilak was member of which of these organisations?
   (a) Madras Native Association
   (b) Puna Sarvjanik Sabha
   (c) East India Association
   (d) India League

5. Who among these freedom fighters became the first Indian to join the Indian Civil Services during British Raj?
   (a) Rabindranath Tagore
   (b) Satyendranath Tagore
   (c) Debendranath Tagore
   (d) Bankimchandra Chatterjee

6. Gopal Krishna Gokhale established which of these organisations at Pune?
   (a) Servants of India Society
   (b) Puna Sarvjanik Sabha
   (c) British India Association
   (d) Landholder's society

7. The Safety Valve Theory of formation of Congress was given by which of these Leaders?
   (a) Lala Lajpat Rai
   (b) Aurobindo Ghosh
   (c) Bankim Chandra Chatterjee
   (d) Mahatma Gandhi

8. Which among the following were the first General Secretary of Indian National Congress?
   (a) W.C. Banerjee
   (b) A.O. Hume
   (c) William Wedderburn
   (d) George Yule

9. W.C. Banerjee was the President of the First Session of INC. Who presided over the Second Session?
   (a) Badruddin Tyabji
   (b) Pherozeshah Mehta
   (c) W.C. Banerjee
   (d) Dadabhai Naoroji

10. Which of these was the first English President of Indian National Congress?
(a) Annie Besant
(b) George Yule
(c) William Wedderburn
(d) A.O Hume

11. Mahatma Gandhi became the President of which of the following sessions of Indian National Congress?
(a) Delhi (b) Belgaum
(c) Kanpur (d) Haripura

12. The Jana Gana Mana was sung for the first time at which of these sessions of Indian National Congress?
(a) Karachi, 1913
(b) Calcutta, 1911
(c) Lucknow, 1916
(d) Belgaum, 1924

13. Which among the following were not a leader of the Moderate phase of INC?
(a) Aurobindo Ghosh
(b) Gopal Krishna Gokhale
(c) Anand Mohan Bose
(d) Madan Mohan Malviya

14. Which of the following Nationalist groups demanded 'Swaraj' from the British for the first time?
(a) Extremists
(b) Moderates
(c) Revolutionaries
(d) Gandhians

15. The Surat Split between Extremist and Moderate groups of Congress took place in which of the following movements?
(a) Civil Disobedience Movement
(b) Non Cooperation Movement
(c) Swadeshi Movement
(d) Quit India Movement

16. Which of the following Newspapers was not published by Mahatma Gandhi?
(a) Indian Opinion
(b) Young India
(c) Navjivan
(d) Kesari

17. Gandhiji had setup a Satyagraha Sabha in 1919 to organise a mass movement against which of the following?
(a) Simon Commission
(b) Rowlatt Act
(c) Jallianwala Bagh Massacre
(d) Zamindars in Kheda

18. In which session, the Congress adopted a resolution for the Non-Cooperation Movement under the leadership of Mahatma Gandhi?
(a) Calcutta Session 1906
(b) Lahore Session 1900
(c) Amritsar Session 1919
(d) Nagpur Session 1920

19. The Congress Khilafat Swaraj Party was formed under the leadership of which among the following leaders?
(a) Mahatma Gandhi
(b) Jawahar Lal Nehru
(c) Bhagat Singh
(d) Chittranjan Das

20. The Simon Commission was setup according to provisions of which of these famous Acts?
(a) Government of India Act, 1935
(b) Indian Councils Act, 1861
(c) Government of India Act, 1919
(d) Indian Councils Act, 1892

21. The Azad Hind Fauj was formed with cooperation of which of these countries?
(a) Germany (b) USSR
(c) USA (d) Japan

2 Marks Questions

22. Which among the following is correctly matched?

	Freedom Fighter	Popular Name
1.	Khan Abdul Ghaffar Khan	Frontier Gandhi
2.	Dadabhai Naoroji	Grand Old Man of India
3.	Bal Gangadhar Tilak	Punjab Kesari

Codes
(a) Only 1
(b) Only 3
(c) Only 1 and 3
(d) Only 1 and 2

23. Arrange the following events in a chronological order.

1. Arrival of Simon Commission
2. Formulation of Mountbatten Plan
3. Partition of Bengal
4. Chauri Chaura Incident

Codes
(a) 1, 2, 4 and 3
(b) 3, 4, 1, 2
(c) 1, 3, 2, 4
(d) 4, 3, 1, 2

24. Match the following.

	List I (Organisation)		List II (Year of Formation)
A.	Indian National Congress	1.	1923
B.	Swaraj Party	2.	1916
C.	Home Rule League	3.	1885
D.	Azad Hind Fauz	4.	1943

Codes

	A	B	C	D		A	B	C	D
(a)	3	1	2	4	(b)	2	3	1	4
(c)	1	3	2	4	(d)	1	2	3	4

25. Which of the following statements is/are true?

1. Subhas Chandra Bose had founded the 'Forward Bloc'.
2. The Ghadar Movement was launched within India by Congress to overthrow the British Rule.
3. Swadeshi Movement was launched as a struggle against the Partition of Bengal in 1905.

Codes
(a) 1 and 2   (b) 2 and 3
(c) 1 and 3   (d) 1, 2 and 3

Chapter 05

World History

1 Mark Questions

1. The Mesopotamian Civilisation was established around which of the following countries in present world?
   (a) Iraq and Kuwait
   (b) Saudi Arabia
   (c) Syria and Lebanon
   (d) Mongolia

2. Chinese Civilisation developed around which of the following rivers?
   (a) Euphrates
   (b) Tigris
   (c) Oxus
   (d) Hwang Ho

3. Which of the following books written by Jacques Rousseau inspired the French Revolution of 1789?
   (a) Das Capital
   (b) The State and Revolution
   (c) The Social Contract
   (d) Mein Kamph

4. Which of these were the main Principles of French Revolution?
   (a) Democracy, Society and Prosperity
   (b) Liberty, Equality and Fraternity
   (c) Peace, Love and Equality
   (d) Social Rights, Political Rights and Human Rights

5. Which of the following Monarchs of France was beheaded after the French Revolution?
   (a) Louis XVI   (b) Louis XIV
   (c) Louis XIII   (d) Louis XVII

6. The American War of Independence began in which of the following year?
   (a) 1795   (b) 1763   (c) 1775   (d) 1781

7. Which of the following organisations were formed for maintaining peace in the World after the First World War?
   (a) United Nations
   (b) The International Organisation for Peace, Care and Relief
   (c) The League of Nations
   (d) Amnesty International

8. Which of the following countries were known as the Sickman of Europe?
   (a) Russia   (b) Germany
   (c) France   (d) Turkey

9. Who among the following was the leader of October revolution of Russia?
   (a) Joseph Stalin
   (b) Vladimir Lenin
   (c) Nikita Khrushchev
   (d) Leonid Brezhnev

10. The policy of 'Iron and Blood' was propounded by which of these German Leaders?
(a) Adolf Hitler
(b) Karl Donitz
(c) Otto von Bismarck
(d) Paul von Hindenburg

11. Which President of Germany appointed Hitler as the Chancellor of Germany?
(a) Hans Luther
(b) Wilhelm Pieck
(c) Karl Donitz
(d) Paul von Hindenberg

12. World War II was fought by Japan under which of the following Emperors?
(a) Akihito
(b) Taisho
(c) Hirohito
(d) Naruhito

13. The Folk Tales One thousand and One nights were contributed by the writers from which of these civilisations?
(a) Mesopotamian Civilisation
(b) Arabian Civilisation
(c) Roman Civilisation
(d) Harappan Civilisation

2 Marks Questions

14. Consider the following statements.
1. The central powers during World War I were Germany, Austria, Hungary, Turkey and Japan.
2. United States entered the World War I from 1917 with an alliance of Britain, France, Russia and Italy.
3. The imperial dynasties of Britain, France and Russia collapsed after the World War I.

Which of the statements given above is/are true?
Codes
(a) Only 1
(b) Only 3
(c) Only 2
(d) Both 1 and 2

15. Match the following.

List I (Events)		List II (Years)
A. American Revolution	1.	1789-1799
B. Russian Revolution	2.	1776-1783
C. French Revolution	3.	1917-1923
D. Chinese Revolution	4.	1945-1949

Codes

	A	B	C	D		A	B	C	D
(a)	3	1	2	4	(b)	2	3	1	4
(c)	1	3	2	4	(d)	1	2	3	4

16. Identify the incorrect match among the following?

	Historical Personality	Country
1.	Napoleon	France
2.	Adolf Hitler	Italy
3.	Karl Marx	Germany

Select the correct answer from the codes given below:
(a) Only 1   (b) Only 2
(c) Only 1 and 3   (d) Only 2 and 3

17. Which of the following factors resulted in the outbreak of World War II?
1. Growth of Militarism in Japan.
2. The French search for security.
3. The rise of communism and its propaganda machinery.

Select the correct answer from the codes given below:
(a) Only 1 and 2   (b) Only 1 and 3
(c) Only 2 and 3   (d) 1, 2 and 3

Chapter 06

Art and Culture

1 Mark Questions

1. The symbol of Swastika has its origin in the art forms of which civilisation?
   (a) Mesopotamian Civilisation
   (b) Indus Valley Civilisation
   (c) Arabian Civilisation
   (d) Chinese Civilisation

2. The popular Hornbill cultural festival is celebrated in which of these states of India?
   (a) Assam
   (b) Gujarat
   (c) Nagaland
   (d) Arunachal Pradesh

3. The Jallikattu festival of Tamil Nadu is famous for which of the following?
   (a) Bull fighting
   (b) Buffalo racing
   (c) Horse racing
   (d) Wrestling

4. The Warli painting is a famous painting form of which of these states?
   (a) Tamil Nadu
   (b) Bihar
   (c) Assam
   (d) Maharashtra

5. Mural paintings are painted on which of the following surfaces?
   (a) Cotton Cloth   (b) Wall or Ceiling
   (c) Synthetic Canvas (d) Paper

6. The Chikankari embroidery is indigenous to which of these places in India?
   (a) Kanpur   (b) Bareilly
   (c) Rayalaseema   (d) Lucknow

7. The oldest rock cut caves in India is ....
   (a) Ajanta Cave   (b) Amarnath Cave
   (c) Badami Cave   (d) Barabar Cave

8. Which of these monuments were built by Allaudin Khilji?
   (a) Tomb of Salim Chishti
   (b) Ala'i Darwaza
   (c) Safdarjung's tomb
   (d) Tomb of Nizamudin Auliya

9. The CharBagh style seen in Mughal era tombs was adopted from which of the following architectural styles?
   (a) Mongolian Architecture
   (b) Persian Architecture
   (c) Greek Architecture
   (d) Victorian Architecture

10. Dandiya folk dance belongs to Gujarat. Lavani folk dance belongs to ....
    (a) Madhya Pradesh (b) Maharashtra
    (c) Andhra Pradesh (d) Uttar Pradesh

11. The Classical Dance form Mohiniyattam belongs to which of these states?
    (a) Uttar Pradesh
    (b) Andhra Pradesh
    (c) Kerala
    (d) Tamil Nadu

12. Kathak is famous dance form of which state?
    (a) Goa   (b) Bihar
    (c) Jharkhand   (d) Uttar Pradesh

13. The largest Hindu temple in India is ....
    (a) Srirangam Temple
    (b) Konark Sun Temple
    (c) Somnath Temple
    (d) Akshardham Temple

2 Marks Questions

14. Which of the following is correctly matched?

	Folk Painting	State
1.	Kalighat	Bihar
2.	Kalamkari	Andhra Pradesh
3.	Paitkar	Jharkhand

    Codes
    (a) Only 1   (b) Only 2 and 3
    (c) Only 1 and 3   (d) Only 3

15. Consider the following statements.
    1. The Zari/zardosi form of embroidery was introduced by Mughals in India.
    2. The Gota form of embroidery originated in Rajasthan.
    3. Phulkari is a embroidery form of Punjab.

    Which of the statements given above is/are true?
    Codes
    (a) Only 1 and 2
    (b) Only 2 and 3
    (c) Only 1 and 3
    (d) All of the above

16. Match the following.

	Folk Dance		Associated with
A.	Jawara	1.	Haryana
B	Jhumar	2.	Rajasthan
C.	Ghoomar	3.	Madhya Pradesh

    Codes

	A	B	C		A	B	C
(a)	1	2	3	(b)	3	1	2
(c)	2	3	1	(d)	1	3	2

Chapter 07

Our Universe and Earth

1 Mark Questions

1. Which of the following astronomers propounded the Big Bang hypothesis of origin of Universe?
   (a) Johaness Kepler
   (b) Edwin Hubble
   (c) Georges Lemaitre
   (d) Fred Hoyle

2. When was the Milky Way Galaxy formed?
   (a) 13 billion years ago
   (b) 5 billion years ago
   (c) 2 billion years ago
   (d) 9 billion years ago

3. The Black Hole at the centre of the Milky Way Galaxy is known as ....
   (a) NGC 1277 (b) Sagittarius A
   (c) Pisces (d) Messier

4. The average temperature of Photosphere of Sun is ....
   (a) 1.5×10^6 °C (b) 6000 °C
   (c) 3 billion °C (d) 2000 °C

5. Which of the following processes is the source of energy of Sun?
   (a) Nuclear Fission (b) Convection
   (c) Radiation (d) Nuclear Fusion

6. Which among the following is the brightest star outside the Solar system?
   (a) Vega (b) Sirius
   (c) Epsilon (d) Proxima Centuari

7. The death explosion of a massive star is known as ....
   (a) Neutron Star (b) Black Hole
   (c) Pulsar (d) Supernova

8. Why is Venus known as Morning Star and Evening Star?
   (a) Nuclear Fusion takes place in its core.
   (b) Its shape is like a star.
   (c) It is the brightest planet.
   (d) It twinkles in the sky during dusk and dawn.

9. Which of these planets rotates in an opposite direction to the Earth?
   (a) Mars (b) Mercury
   (c) Uranus (d) Jupiter

10. Which of these planets has no natural Moons?
    (a) Mars and Venus
    (b) Mercury and Venus
    (c) Uranus and Neptune
    (d) Jupiter and Saturn

11. The largest natural satellite of the solar system is ....
    (a) Deimos
    (b) Phobos
    (c) Callisto
    (d) Ganymede

12. Neptune makes one complete revolution around Sun in how many Earth years?
    (a) 1.5 years
    (b) 164.8 years
    (c) 200 years
    (d) 2.5 years

13. In 2006, Pluto was classified as a Dwarf planet, who discovered Pluto?
    (a) Galileo Galilei
    (b) Albert Einstein
    (c) Plato
    (d) Clyde Tombaugh

14. The Halley's comet is visible from the Earth after how many years?
    (a) 1000 years
    (b) 365 years
    (c) 76 years
    (d) 100 years

15. 0° (Zero) Longitude passes through which of these famous places?
    (a) Manhattan
    (b) Greenwich
    (c) Brooklyn
    (d) Mecca

16. Which among these is the most abundant element in Earth's Crust?
    (a) Iron and Nickel
    (b) Aluminium and Magnesium
    (c) Silicon and Oxygen
    (d) Calcium and Sodium

17. Which of the following layers of Earth has least density?
    (a) Inner Core
    (b) Mantle
    (c) Asthenosphere
    (d) Crust

18. Which of the following is true about Earth?
    (a) The shape of Earth is a perfect sphere.
    (b) Earth rotates on its axis at an inclination of 23°.
    (c) Equatorial radius of Earth is 12742 km.
    (d) 29% of Earth's surface is covered with water.

19. The Lithosphere inside the Earth consists of which of the following?
    (a) Outer Core + Lower Mantle
    (b) Inner Core + Outer Core
    (c) Crust + Upper Mantle
    (d) Continental Crust + Oceanic Crust

20. The Continental Crust of Earth is made up of which of these elements?
    (a) Aluminium and Oxygen
    (b) Silicon and Oxygen
    (c) Silicon and Aluminium
    (d) Iron and Nickle

21. Which of these layers of Earth is also known as SI-MA layer?
    (a) Oceanic Crust
    (b) Continental Crust
    (c) Inner Core
    (d) Mantle

22. Which layer of the atmosphere contains 90% of all the gases present on Earth?
    (a) Mesosphere
    (b) Stratosphere
    (c) Ionosphere
    (d) Troposphere

23. Which among the following layers of Earth gradually merges with the outer space?
    (a) Thermosphere
    (b) Exosphere
    (c) Stratosphere
    (d) Mesosphere

24. The diameter of Moon is what percentage of the diameter of Earth?
    (a) 50 %
    (b) 25 %
    (c) 75 %
    (d) 15 %

25. The distance between Earth and Moon is ....
    (a) 1.5 million km
    (b) 15 Lakh km
    (c) 2×10^5 km
    (d) 3.84 Lakh km

2 Marks Questions

26. Which of these statements is/are correct?

    1. Jovian planets are made up of rocks and metals.
    2. Only Mars and Earth are Jovian planets.
    3. Among all the planets, Earth has highest density.

    Codes
    (a) Only 1 and 2   (b) Only 1 and 3
    (c) Only 2   (d) Only 3

27. Which of the following are true regarding asteroids?

    1. Asteroids revolve around the Sun.
    2. Asteroid belt is located between orbits of Mars and Earth.
    3. The largest known asteroid is Ceres.

    Codes
    (a) Only 1 and 3
    (b) 1, 2 and 3
    (c) Only 1 and 2
    (d) None of the above

28. Which of the following statements is/are true about the Earth?

    1. The Mantle of the Earth constitutes 85% of the volume of Earth.
    2. Magma is mainly present in the Mantle of Earth.
    3. The Mantle is second thickest layer of Earth's interior.

    Codes
    (a) Only 1 and 2   (b) Only 1 and 3
    (c) Only 1   (d) Only 3 and 2

29. Which of the following statements is/are true?

    1. All the longitudes converge at the Poles on the surface of Earth.
    2. As we move from Equator to Poles, the distance between latitudes decreases.
    3. 180° longitude is known as International Date Line.

    Codes
    (a) Only 1   (b) Only 3
    (c) Only 1 and 3   (d) All of these

Chapter 08

Continents

1 Mark Questions

1. Asia is the largest continent of the world. Which is the second largest?
   (a) North America
   (b) South America
   (c) Europe
   (d) Africa

2. Which of these mountain ranges is not located in Asia?
   (a) Arakan Mountain
   (b) Karakoram Range
   (c) Alps Mountain
   (d) Tien Shan Range

3. Which of these is the highest peak of Karakoram mountain range located in Asia?
   (a) Mt. Godwin Austen
   (b) Mt. Everest
   (c) Mt. Gasherbrum
   (d) Mt. Kilimanjaro

4. Which of the following is the largest plateau of Asia?
   (a) Iran Plateau
   (b) Antolian Plateau
   (c) Tibetan Plateau
   (d) Arabian Plateau

5. Which of the following is the longest river in Asia?
   (a) Brahmaputra River
   (b) Mekong River
   (c) Hwang Ho River
   (d) Yangtse River

6. Which of these is the largest lake of the world?
   (a) Lake Superior   (b) Lake Baikal
   (c) Caspian Sea   (d) Lake Van

7. Russia is the largest country in Asia, which is the second largest?
   (a) India   (b) Saudi Arabia
   (c) Iraq   (d) China

8. Which of these is the highest peak of the continent of Africa?
   (a) Mt. Kenya   (b) Mt. Cameroon
   (c) Mt. Kilimanjaro   (d) Mt. Etna

9. The African Continent does not border which of the following seas/oceans?
   (a) Red Sea
   (b) Atlantic Ocean
   (c) Mediterranean Sea
   (d) Caspian Sea

10. Appalachian mountain range, one of the world's oldest mountain is located in which country?
    (a) Canada   (b) U.S.A
    (c) Mexico   (d) Chile

11. Which of these countries has the largest coastline in the world?
    (a) China   (b) Japan
    (c) Canada   (d) Chile

12. Which one of the following is an active volcano in South America?
    (a) Mt. Stromboli
    (b) Mt. Etna
    (c) Mt. Cotopaxi
    (d) Mt. Krakatoa

13. The longest mountain range of the world is
    (a) Tien Shan   (b) The Rocky
    (c) The Himalayas   (d) The Andes

14. South America and North America are connected to each other by which of these?
    (a) Kra Isthumus
    (b) Panama Isthumus
    (c) Suez Isthumus
    (d) Gibraltar Isthumus

15. Which among the following is the longest river in Europe?
    (a) Elbe   (b) Danube
    (c) Rhine   (d) Volga

16. Which of these countries occupies the largest land area in Europe after Russia?
    (a) France   (b) Germany
    (c) Spain   (d) Sweden

17. Europe is separated from Asia by which of these mountain range?
    (a) Mt. Elbrus
    (b) Ural Mountains
    (c) Applachian Mountain
    (d) Pontic Mountain

18. Alps mountain range forms a border between which of these countries?
    (a) France and Germany
    (b) Italy and France
    (c) Spain and France
    (d) Ukraine and Russia

19. The Great Barrier Reef, world's largest coral reef is located along the coast of which of these countries?
    (a) Indonesia
    (b) New Zealand
    (c) Australia
    (d) Madagascar

20. The world's largest glacier is located in Antarctica. The name of the Glacier is ....
    (a) Aletsch Glacier
    (b) Lambert Glacier
    (c) Fedchenko Glacier
    (d) Upsala Glacier

2 Marks Questions

21. Which of the following statements is/are true about the Atacama Desert?

1. It is the world's driest desert.
2. It is bordered by the Indian Ocean.
3. It is located in Chile.

Codes
(a) Only 1   (b) Only 1 and 2
(c) Only 1 and 3   (d) Only 2

22. Which of the following statements is/are true?

1. Antarctica is the largest cold desert of the world.
2. Kalahari Desert is the largest hot desert of the world.
3. The Continent of Europe does not contain any desert.

Codes
(a) Only 1   (b) Only 1 and 3
(c) 1, 2 and 3   (d) Only 2 and 3

23. Which of the following statements are true?

1. The Continent of Africa is also known as Dark Continent.
2. South America is the fourth largest continent of the world.
3. Europe is the smallest continent of the world in terms of area.

Codes
(a) Only 1 and 3   (b) Only 1, 2 and 3
(c) Only 1 and 2   (d) All of these

24. Arrange the following continents in terms of their size from smallest to largest?

1. Africa   2. Europe
3. Antarctica   4. South America

Codes
(a) 1- 2- 3- 4   (b) 2- 1- 3- 4
(c) 2- 3- 4- 1   (d) 3- 2- 1- 4

25. Match the following.

	List I (River)		List II (Flows in)
A.	Mississippi	1.	North America
B.	Zaire	2.	Asia
C.	Mekong	3.	Africa

Codes

	A	B	C			A	B	C
(a)	1	2	3		(b)	3	1	2
(c)	1	3	2		(d)	2	1	3

26. Match the following.

	List I (Water Falls)		List II (Located in)
A.	Angel Falls	1.	South America
B.	Niagra Falls	2.	Africa
C.	Blue Nile Falls	3.	North America

Codes

	A	B	C			A	B	C
(a)	2	3	1		(b)	1	3	2
(c)	3	2	1		(d)	1	2	3

India : Size, Location and Physical Features

1 Mark Questions

1. The rank of India in terms of its area in the world is ....
   (a) third   (b) second
   (c) seventh   (d) sixth

2. The southernmost point of India is Kanyakumari, which is the northernmost Point?
   (a) Indira Point   (b) Kibithu
   (c) Siachen   (d) Indira Kol

3. Which of these major latitudes divide India into almost two equal halves?
   (a) $23\frac{1}{2}^{\circ}$ S   (b) $23\frac{1}{2}^{\circ}$ N
   (c) $66\frac{1}{2}^{\circ}$ N   (d) 45° N

4. The Standard Meridian of India passes through which of these places in India?
   (a) Gorakhpur   (b) Mirzapur
   (c) Vaishali   (d) Vijayanagar

5. India does not share its land border with which of the following countries?
   (a) Myanmar   (b) Afghanistan
   (c) Bhutan   (d) Thailand

6. The Palk Strait separates which of the following countries from India?
   (a) Singapore   (b) Indonesia
   (c) Sri Lanka   (d) Maldives

7. India shares its smallest land border with which of these countries?
   (a) Pakistan   (b) Nepal
   (c) Bhutan   (d) Afghanistan

8. The largest land border of India is ....
   (a) India China Border
   (b) India Bangladesh Border
   (c) India Pakistan Border
   (d) India Nepal Border

9. Which state of India shares longest border with Nepal?
   (a) Uttarakhand
   (b) Himachal Pradesh
   (c) Uttar Pradesh
   (d) Bihar

10. The highest peak of greater Himalayas located in India is ....
    (a) Godwin Austen   (b) Mount Everest
    (c) Kangchenjunga (d) Nanga Parbat

11. Which among the following is also known as The White Mountain?
    (a) Mt. Makalu   (b) Dhaulagiri
    (c) Nanda Devi   (d) Namcha Barwa

12. The Rohtang Pass located in Himachal Pradesh is on which of the following mountain ranges?
    (a) Ladhakh Range
    (b) Karakoram Range
    (c) Kailash Range
    (d) Pir Panjal Range

13. The Himalayan mountain range between Indus and Satluj river is also known by what name?
    (a) Assam Himalayas
    (b) Himachal Himalayas
    (c) Punjab Himalayas
    (d) Kumaon Himalayas

14. The highest peak of South India is ....
    (a) Kamet   (b) Guru Shikhar
    (c) Dhupgarh   (d) Anaimudi

15. The Eastern Ghats and Western Ghats meet at which of these ranges?
    (a) Cardamom Hills
    (b) Satpura Range
    (c) Nilgiri Hills
    (d) Garo Hills

16. Which of the following mountain ranges separates North India from South India?
    (a) Satpura Range
    (b) Vindhayan Range
    (c) Aravalli Range
    (d) Rajmahal Hills

17. Which of these is the oldest mountain in India?
    (a) Western Ghats   (b) Purvanchal Hills
    (c) Aravalli   (d) Himadri

18. Which among the following is the Southernmost mountain in the Indian Peninsula?
    (a) Satpura Range   (b) Anaimalai Hills
    (c) Cardamon Hills (d) Ajanta Hills

19. The Great plains of India are made up of which of the following types of soil?
    (a) Red Soil   (b) Alluvial Soil
    (c) Black Soil   (d) Yellow Soil

20. Which among the following is not true regarding Great Plains of India?
    (a) The Great Plains of India are made up of sand, silt and clay brought by Himalayan rivers.
    (b) The newly formed plains are called Khadar.
    (c) Great Plains are older than the Himalayas.
    (d) Thar is the Westernmost region of Great Plains.

21. Which among these is the largest plateau in India?
    (a) Chhattisgarh Plateau
    (b) Deccan Plateau
    (c) Rayalseema Plateau
    (d) Chota Nagpur Plateau

22. Which among the following plateau is described as the Ruhr of India?
    (a) Karnataka Plateau
    (b) Deccan Plateau
    (c) Chota Nagpur Plateau
    (d) Rayalseema Plateau

23. Which of the following is the largest delta of India?
    (a) Krishna-Godavari Delta
    (b) Mahanadi River Delta
    (c) Sundarban Delta
    (d) Kaveri River Delta

24. Which of these is a Saline lake of India?
(a) Lake Wular   (b) Loktak Lake
(c) Lake Sambar   (d) Lake Pangong

25. The famous backwaters of Kerala, popularly known as Kayals are located on which of these coasts?
(a) Utkal Coast   (b) Coromandal Coast
(c) Malabar Coast   (d) Konkan Coast

26. The only active volcano of India is located on ....
(a) Barren Island
(b) Narcondam Island
(c) Amindivi Island
(d) Colaba Island

27. The Southernmost Point of Indian Islands is located on which of the following Islands?
(a) Little Nicobar Island
(b) Little Andaman Island
(c) Great Nicobar Island
(d) Car Nicobar Island

28. The Eight Degree Channel separates Lakshdweep Island from which of these countries?
(a) Sri Lanka
(b) Madagascar
(c) Maldives
(d) Indonesia

2 Marks Questions

29. Consider the following statements.
1. The Lakshdweep Islands are Coral in origin.
2. The Andaman and Nicobar Islands are an extension of Arakanyoma Range.
3. The only active volcano of South Asia is in Andaman and Nicobar Islands.

Codes
(a) Only 1   (b) Only 2
(c) Only 1 and 3   (d) All of these

30. Match the following.

List I (Coastal Area)		List II (State)
A.	Konkan Coast	1. Tamil Nadu
B.	Northern Circar	2. Goa
C.	Coromandel Coast	3. Odisha

Codes

	A	B	C		A	B	C
(a)	2	3	1	(b)	1	2	3
(c)	3	1	2	(d)	2	1	3

31. Match the following.

List I (Lake)		List II (Located in)
A.	Loktak Lake	1. Manipur
B.	Chilika Lake	2. Rajasthan
C.	Bhimtal Lake	3. Odisha
D.	Pushkar Lake	4. Uttarakhand

Codes

	A	B	C	D		A	B	C	D
(a)	4	1	2	3	(b)	1	4	2	3
(c)	1	2	4	3	(d)	1	3	4	2

India Drainage and Climate

1 Mark Questions

1. The Indus River originates from which of the following places?
   (a) Kailash Mountain
   (b) Pir Panjal Mountain
   (c) Karakoram Range
   (d) Kullu Hills

2. Which of these is the largest tributary of Indus?
   (a) Ravi
   (b) Chenab
   (c) Jhelum
   (d) Beas

3. The Alaknanda and Bhagirathi River meet at which of the following places?
   (a) Karna Prayag
   (b) Rudra Prayag
   (c) Dev Prayag
   (d) Nand Prayag

4. Which among the following is the largest tributary of River Ganga?
   (a) Bhagirathi
   (b) Yamuna
   (c) Dhauli Ganga
   (d) Son

5. Which among the following rivers form ravines or Badlands in Madhya Pradesh?
   (a) Son
   (b) Narmada
   (c) Chambal
   (d) Mahi

6. River Kosi is known as the Sorrow of Bihar, which of these rivers was known as the Sorrow of Bengal?
   (a) Mahanadi
   (b) Damodar
   (c) Ghaghra
   (d) Gandak

7. The Brahmaputra River does not pass through which of these states of India?
   (a) Arunachal Pradesh
   (b) Assam
   (c) Meghalaya
   (d) Both (a) and (c)

8. Which among the following rivers drain into the Bay of Bengal?
   (a) Narmada
   (b) Sabarmati
   (c) Mahanadi
   (d) Luni

9. Which among the following rivers is a major tributary of Godavari?
   (a) Hooghly
   (b) Lohit
   (c) Penganga
   (d) Tista

10. Which among the following rivers flows through the rift valley of Satpuras?
    (a) Sabarmati
    (b) Luni
    (c) Mahanadi
    (d) Narmada

11. India receives more than 75 % of its annual rainfall from which of the following rain systems?
(a) South West Monsoon
(b) North East Monsoon
(c) Western Disturbances
(d) Both (b) and (c)

12. The North East monsoon winds cause rainfall in which of these states during winters?
(a) Goa
(b) Uttar Pradesh
(c) Kerala
(d) Tamil Nadu

13. The upper air tropospheric circulation during the Monsoon season of India is known as ....
(a) Western Disturbance
(b) Cyclone
(c) Jet Stream
(d) Tropospheric Stream

14. The season of October heat is characterised by which among the following conditions in India?
(a) High Temperature, Low Humidity
(b) Low Temperature, Low Humidity
(c) High Temperature, High Humidity
(d) Low Temperature, High Humidity

2 Marks Questions

15. Arrange the following rivers of India from North to South.
1. Cauvery
2. Narmada
3. Krishna
4. Godavari

Codes
(a) 1, 2, 3, 4
(b) 2, 4, 3, 1
(c) 4, 3, 2, 1
(d) 1, 3, 2, 4

16. Match the following.

	River		Origin
A.	Ganga	1.	Madhya Pradesh
B.	Narmada	2.	Uttarakhand
C.	Mahanadi	3.	Chhattisgarh

Codes

	A	B	C
(a)	2	1	3
(b)	3	1	2
(c)	2	3	1
(d)	1	3	2

17. Which of the following is correctly matched?

	River	Tributary
1.	Ganga	Gandak
2.	Yamuna	Chambal
3.	Brahmaputra	Bhagirathi
4.	Narmada	Tista

Codes
(a) Only 1 and 3   (b) Only 2 and 4
(c) Only 1 and 2   (d) Only 1 and 4

16. Which of the following statement(s) is/are correct with respect to Indian drainage system?
1. The Ganga enters the plain at Haridwar.
2. The river Mahanadi originates in Himalaya.
3. The Peninsular rivers are perennial.

Select the correct answer from the codes given below:
(a) Only 1   (b) Only 2
(c) Only 3   (d) 1, 2 and 3

India: Land, Soil and Water Resources

1 Mark Questions

1. The largest share of land in India is constituted by which of these features?
   (a) Mountains   (b) Plains
   (c) Plateaus   (d) Deltas

2. Which of these categories constitute the second largest land use in India?
   (a) Barren Land
   (b) Forest Land
   (c) Fallow Land
   (d) Permanent Pasture Land

3. Which of the following lands is a culturable wasteland in India?
   (a) Land uncultivated for less than 1 year
   (b) Land uncultivated for more than 5 years
   (c) Land under forest cover
   (d) Land used for pasture and grazing

4. Which of these states has the largest area under forest cover?
   (a) Arunachal Pradesh
   (b) Madhya Pradesh
   (c) Assam
   (d) Himachal Pradesh

5. Which of the following is the main reason for degradation of land in states such as Jharkhand, Madhya Pradesh and Odisha?
   (a) Over grazing
   (b) Over irrigation
   (c) Mining and quarrying
   (d) Urban sprawl

6. Which among the following is an organic material in soil that improves its fertility?
   (a) Clay   (b) Potassium
   (c) Humus   (d) Nitrogen

7. Alluvial soil is mainly found in which of these places in India?
   (a) Mountain Region
   (b) Terai Region
   (c) Coastal Deltas
   (d) Both (b) and (c)

8. Which of these soils constitute the largest proportion of land area of India?
   (a) Black Soil   (b) Alluvial Soil
   (c) Laterite Soil   (d) Red Soil

9. Which of the following type of soils is most suitable for cultivation of cotton?
   (a) Alluvial Soil   (b) Regur Soil
   (c) Laterite Soil   (d) Red Soil

10. The black soil is made up of which of the following?
    (a) Silt and Clay   (b) Igneous Lava
    (c) Sand   (d) Granite

11. The Red and Yellow soils are reddish in colour because presence of ....
(a) Calcium
(b) Phosphate
(c) Iron
(d) Silicate

12. Which of these soil requires high amount of fertilisers for making them suitable for cultivation?
(a) Alluvial Soil
(b) Laterite Soil
(c) Black Soil
(d) Red Soil

13. Which among the following soils are acidic in nature?
(a) Black Soil
(b) Alluvial Soil
(c) Laterite Soil
(d) Yellow Soil

14. Which of these state has the largest area under Arid soil?
(a) Arunachal Pradesh
(b) Haryana
(c) Rajasthan
(d) Maharashtra

15. Which of these water sources contributes the largest proportion to irrigation in India?
(a) Rivers
(b) Ground Water
(c) Fresh Water Lakes
(d) Sea Water

16. The Tehri Dam in Uttarakhand is built on which of these rivers?
(a) Alaknanda
(b) Dhauli Ganga
(c) Kali
(d) Bhagirathi

17. The Indira Gandhi Canal is fed by which among the following dams?
(a) Pong Dam
(b) Tehri Dam
(c) Bhakra Dam
(d) Sardar Sarovar

18. Which of the following methods or irrigation can help in conservation of water resources?
(a) Tank Irrigation
(b) Tubewell Irrigation
(c) Drip Irrigation
(d) Canal Irrigation

2 Marks Questions

19. Which of the following techniques can reduce soil erosion?

    1. Mulching

    2. Terrace cultivation

    3. Shelter plantations

Codes
(a) Only 1
(b) Only 3
(c) Only 2 and 3
(d) All of these

20. Match the following.

Dam		River	
A.	Sardar Sarovar	1.	Ganga
B.	Farakka Dam	2.	Narmada
C.	Bhakra Dam	3.	Sutlej

Codes

	A	B	C		A	B	C
(a)	1	3	2	(b)	2	3	1
(c)	1	2	3	(d)	2	1	3

21. Match the following.

Soil		Found in	
A.	Alluvial Soil	1.	Deccan Plateau
B.	Black Soil	2.	Krishna Delta
C.	Arid Soil	3.	Thar Region

Codes

	A	B	C		A	B	C
(a)	1	2	3	(b)	2	1	3
(c)	2	3	1	(d)	1	3	2

India : Minerals and Energy Resources

1 Mark Questions

1. Which among the following is a non-metallic mineral found in India?
   (a) Lead   (b) Bauxite
   (c) Nickel   (d) Mica

2. Minerals can be found in which of the following type of rocks?
   (a) Metamorphic rocks
   (b) Igneous rocks
   (c) Sedimentary rocks
   (d) All of the above

3. Which among the following minerals is a placer deposit?
   (a) Copper   (b) Coal
   (c) Gold   (d) Uranium

4. The highest quality of iron ore is Magnetite, which of these has the second highest quality?
   (a) Limonite   (b) Haematite
   (c) Geothite   (d) Ilmenite

5. Which state has the highest reserves of Iron ore in India?
   (a) Odisha
   (b) Madhya Pradesh
   (c) Jharkhand
   (d) Goa

6. Which of these minerals is used for manufacturing of steel?
   (a) Mica   (b) Bauxite
   (c) Manganese   (d) Cobalt

7. Which of these states has the largest reserves of copper in India?
   (a) Jharkhand   (b) Madhya Pradesh
   (c) Odisha   (d) Rajasthan

8. Which among the following minerals is an important raw material in the Cement Industry?
   (a) Lead   (b) Granite
   (c) Sulphur   (d) Limestone

9. Which among the following is the most abundant fossil fuel found in India?
   (a) Petroleum   (b) Shale
   (c) Coal   (d) Natural Gas

10. Which among the following is the highest quality Coal?
    (a) Lignite   (b) Peat
    (c) Bituminous   (d) Anthracite

11. The major coal resources of India are found in which of the following types?
    (a) Lignite Deposit   (b) Gondwana Deposit
    (c) Tertiary Deposit   (d) Both (a) and (c)

12. Which of these is the first petroleum producing state of India?
(a) Meghalaya   (b) Kerala
(c) Assam   (d) Maharashtra

13. Which of these is the largest petroleum refinery of India?
(a) Digboi   (b) Mumbai High
(c) Jamnagar   (d) Kochi

14. The largest reserves of Thorium are found in the Monazite sand of which of these states?
(a) Odisha   (b) Madhya Pradesh
(c) Rajasthan   (d) Kerala

15. The Tarapur Atomic power station was established in which of these states?
(a) Rajasthan
(b) Maharashtra
(c) Haryana
(d) Assam

16. Which among the following is a Non-Conventional source of Energy?
(a) Thermal Electricity
(b) Hydroelectricity
(c) Tidal Energy
(d) Fossil Fuels

2 Marks Questions

17. Consider the following statements.
1. Mica is found in the Chhotanagpur plateau.
2. Mica is used as an insulator in the Electrical Industry.

Which of the statements given above is/are true?
Codes
(a) Only 1   (b) Only 2
(c) Both 1 and 2   (d) None of these

18. Consider the following statements.
1. The Gulf of Kachchh region is ideal for producing Tidal Energy.
2. Gujarat and Tamil Nadu have enormous potential for Wind Energy.

Which of the statements given above is/are true?
Codes
(a) Only 1   (b) Only 2
(c) Both 1 and 2   (d) None of these

19. Consider the following statements.
1. Natural gas emits lower carbon dioxide than petroleum.
2. Diesel fuel is more polluting than Petrol.

3. Vehicles running on CNG produce less pollution than diesel cars.

Which of the statements given above is/are true?
Codes
(a) Only 1   (b) Only 2
(c) Only 1 and 3   (d) All of these

20. Which of these is a coal mining region in India?
1. Jharia   2. Bokaro
3. Barauni   4. Mumbai High
Codes
(a) Only 1   (b) Only 2
(c) Only 1 and 2   (d) All of the above

21. Match the following correctly.

	Iron Mine		State
A.	Mayurbhanj	1.	Maharashtra
B.	Ratnagiri	2.	Karnataka
C.	Chikamanglore	3.	Odisha

Codes

	A	B	C		A	B	C
(a)	1	2	3	(b)	2	1	3
(c)	2	3	1	(d)	3	1	2

India : Agriculture

1 Mark Questions

1. Jhumming or Shifting cultivation is still practised in India in which of the following regions?
   (a) Punjab and Haryana
   (b) Rajasthan and Madhya Pradesh
   (c) Nagaland and Mizoram
   (d) Kerala and Tamil Nadu

2. Plantation agriculture is characterised by which among the following?
   (a) Small landholdings
   (b) Growing single crop
   (c) Use of traditional seeds
   (d) Use of large machines

3. Which among the following is a commercial crop?
   (a) Coffee (b) Rice (c) Millets (d) Ragi

4. Which of these crops is a Horticultural Crop?
   (a) Maize   (b) Barley
   (c) Bananas   (d) Lentils

5. The period of October-November is characterised by which of these agricultural seasons?
   (a) Zaid Sowing Season
   (b) Kharif Sowing Season
   (c) Rabi Sowing Season
   (d) None of the above

6. Which among the following is a Rabi Crop?
   (a) Maize   (b) Rice
   (c) Soybean   (d) Wheat

7. Which of these is a crop that is sown in the Zaid season?
   (a) Cucumber   (b) Watermelon
   (c) Vegetables   (d) All of these

8. Parmal, Sharbati, Basmati and Sona are types of which of the following crops in India?
   (a) Wheat   (b) Maize
   (c) Jowar   (d) Rice

9. Which among the following states produces largest amount of rice in India?
   (a) Jharkhand   (b) Madhya Pradesh
   (c) Maharashtra   (d) West Bengal

10. Which among the following is the largest wheat producer of India?
    (a) Madhya Pradesh (b) Kerala
    (c) Assam   (d) Uttar Pradesh

11. Which among the following crop is grown in large plantations?
    (a) Pulses   (b) Rice
    (c) Maize   (d) Tea

12. Which among the following is the largest producer of sugarcane in India?
(a) Rajasthan   (b) Odisha
(c) Tamil Nadu   (d) Uttar Pradesh

13. Arabica and Robusta are varieties of which of the following crops grown in India?
(a) Tea   (b) Sugarcane
(c) Coffee   (d) Malt

14. Coffee is mainly produced in which of the following regions in India?
(a) Garo Hills   (b) Himalayas
(c) Nilgiri Hills   (d) Darjeeling

15. Rearing of Silk Worms for producing Silk is known as ....
(a) Pisiculture   (b) Sericulture
(c) Aviculture   (d) Horticulture

2 Marks Questions

16. Consider the following statements.
1. The crops grown in Primitive subsistence agriculture are Rice, Maize and Beans.
2. The crops grown in Intensive subsistence farming are Rice and Wheat.

Which of the statements given above is/are true?
Codes
(a) Only 2   (b) Only 1
(c) Both 1 and 2   (d) None of these

17. Which of the following is/are true regarding Plantation Agriculture?
1. Transport and Communication networks play an important role in Plantation Agriculture.
2. Plantation agriculture is a form of commercial form of agriculture.
3. Wheat, Maize and Paddy are important crops of Plantations.
Codes
(a) Only 1   (b) Only 1 and 3
(c) Only 1 and 2   (d) All of these

18. Which of the following statements is/are true?
1. Jute is also known as Golden Fibre.
2. The largest producer of Jute in India is Tamil Nadu.
3. Jute is used for making ropes, bags and artefacts.
Codes
(a) Only 1
(b) Only 1 and 3
(c) Only 3
(d) Only 2 and 3

19. Which among the following is correct?
1. Tea plantations were introduced by the British in India.
2. Tea Plantations are grown on the slopes of mountain and foothills.
3. India is the largest producer of Tea in the world.
Codes
(a) Only 2 and 3
(b) Only 1 and 2
(c) Only 1 and 3
(d) All of these

20. Match the following.

	Type of Agriculture		Associated with
A.	Floriculture	1.	Flowers
B.	Apiculture	2.	Bee Keeping
C.	Viticulture	3.	Grape Farming

Codes

	A	B	C			A	B	C
(a)	1	2	3		(b)	2	1	3
(c)	2	3	1		(d)	1	3	2

Chapter 14

India : Industries

1 Mark Questions

1. Which among the following is an agro based industry?
   (a) Petrochemicals industry
   (b) Cement industry
   (c) Rubber industry
   (d) Ship building

2. Which among the following is classified as a basic industry?
   (a) Sugar industry
   (b) Machine tool industry
   (c) Iron and Steel industry
   (d) Paper industry

3. Which among the following is a Private Sector Industry of India?
   (a) Wipro Ltd
   (b) Coal India Ltd
   (c) Bharat Electronics Ltd
   (d) Antrix Corporation

4. Which among the following can be classified as a consumer goods industry?
   (a) Petrochemicals   (b) Paper industry
   (c) Cement industry (d) Coal industry

5. The first mechanised paper mill was setup at which place?
   (a) Kanpur   (b) Barauni
   (c) Serampur   (d) Murshidabad

6. Which among the following was the very first steel plant of India?
   (a) Tata Iron and Steel Plant
   (b) Rourkela Steel Plant
   (c) Indian Iron and Steel Company
   (d) Salem Steel Company

7. Which among the following is the largest steel producer of India?
   (a) JSW Steel Ltd
   (b) Jindal Steel Ltd
   (c) Tata Steel Ltd
   (d) Ambika Steel Ltd

8. The first cotton textile mill of India was setup at which among the following places?
   (a) Ahmedabad   (b) Bombay
   (c) Jaunpur   (d) Kanpur

9. Which among the following is a cotton textile manufacturing centre in West Bengal?
   (a) Jalgaon   (b) Wardha
   (c) Moradabad   (d) Murshidabad

10. The Jute industry of India has declined due to competition from which of these industries?
   (a) Rubber industry (b) Synthetic fibres
   (c) Cotton textiles   (d) Woollen textile

11. The first Jute mill of India was setup in which of these cities?
(a) Amritsar
(b) Bombay
(c) Kolkata
(d) Lucknow

12. Which among the following is known as the Electronics Capital of India?

(a) Mysuru
(b) Hyderabad
(c) Bengaluru
(d) Noida

13. Which among the following is related with IT and Electronics Industry?
(a) Smelting
(b) Business Process Outsourcing
(c) Anti-dumping
(d) Import Substitution

2 Marks Questions

14. Which among the following is/are correctly matched?

Iron and Steel Plant	State
1. Raurkela Steel Plant	Andhra Pradesh
2. Bokaro Steel Plant	Jharkhand
3. Durgapur Steel Plant	West Bengal

Codes
(a) Only 2
(b) Only 2 and 3
(c) Only 1 and 2
(d) Only 1

15. Which of the following is correctly matched?

Type of Industry	Example
1. Private Sector Industry	Tata Steels
2. Public Sector Industry	Bharat Heavy Electronics Ltd.
3. Joint Sector Industry	Bharat Sanchar Nigam Ltd.

Codes
(a) Only 1
(b) Only 1 and 3
(c) Only 1 and 2
(d) Only 3

16. Match the following.

	Industry		Type
A.	Woollen Textile	1.	Mineral based Industry
B.	Aluminium	2.	Consumer goods Industry
C.	Food and Beverage	3.	Agro based Industry

Codes

	A	B	C			A	B	C
(a)	1	2	3		(b)	2	1	3
(c)	2	3	1		(d)	1	3	2

India : Transport and Communication

1 Mark Questions

1. Which among the following type of roads constitute the highest proportion of Road Network in India?
(a) State Highways
(b) Rural Roads
(c) National Highways
(d) District Roads

2. Which among the following states has the highest road length in India?
(a) Tamil Nadu
(b) Uttar Pradesh
(c) Punjab
(d) Maharashtra

3. Which among the following state has the highest density of roads in India?
(a) Sikkim
(b) Uttarakhand
(c) Himachal Pradesh
(d) Kerala

4. The first train in India ran between which among the following places?
(a) Bombay to Pune
(b) Kolkata to Hooghly
(c) Bombay to Thane
(d) Kanpur to Agra

5. How many railway zones are there in India?
(a) 24   (b) 18   (c) 16   (d) 9

6. The headquarters of South-Eastern railways is located at which of these places?
(a) Chennai   (b) Kolkata
(c) Jaipur   (d) Mumbai

7. Which among the following was the first mountain railway of India?
(a) Kalka Shimla Railway
(b) Darjeeling Railway
(c) Nilgiri Railway
(d) Kangra Valley Railway

8. The National Highways (NH) in India is maintained by ....
(a) Central Government
(b) State Government
(c) Both (a) and (b)
(d) None of the above

9. The Hazira-Jagdishpur pipeline transports natural gas between which states?
(a) Madhya Pradesh-Jharkhand
(b) Bihar-Gujarat
(c) Andhra Pradesh-Tamil Nadu
(d) Gujarat-Uttar Pradesh

10. The National Waterway II is located on which among the following rivers?
    (a) Godavari   (b) Ganga
    (c) Brahmaputra   (d) Cauvery

11. Which among the following are most suitable for construction of Inland Waterways?
    (a) Lakes   (b) Rivers
    (c) Canals   (d) All of these

12. Which among the following sea ports were developed as an alternative to Karachi Sea Port after independence?
    (a) Mumbai Sea Port
    (b) Kandla Sea Port
    (c) Chennai Sea Port
    (d) Marmagao Sea Port

13. Which among the following is the deepest sea port of India?
    (a) Kolkata Port
    (b) Haldia Port
    (c) Vishakhapatnam Port
    (d) Tuticorin Port

14. Which among the following is a Tidal Port on the East Coast?
    (a) Chennai Port
    (b) Vishakhapatnam Port
    (c) Kolkata Port
    (d) Paradwip Port

15. Kempegowda international airport is located in which of the following cities?
    (a) Chennai   (b) Hyderabad
    (c) Bengaluru   (d) Mumbai

2 Marks Questions

16. Which among the following statements is/are true?

    1. Road transport is most economical for carrying freight over short distances.
    2. Railways is most economical for carrying large volume of Cargo over long distance.

    Codes
    (a) Only 1   (b) Only 2
    (c) Both 1 and 2   (d) None of these

17. Which among the following cities are connected by the Golden Quadrilateral?
    1. Chennai   2. Mumbai
    3. Delhi   4. Kolkata

    Codes
    (a) Only 1, 2 and 4
    (b) Only 1, 3 and 4
    (c) Only 1, 2 and 3
    (d) All of the above

18. Which of the following is correctly matched?

	Railway Zone	Headquarter
1.	Central Railway	Mumbai
2.	Northern Railway	Delhi
3.	Southern Railway	Vishakhapatnam

Codes
(a) Only 1   (b) Only 3
(c) Only 1 and 2   (d) Only 2 and 3

19. Match the following.

	Sea Port		Located in
A.	Jawaharlal Nehru Port	1.	Karnataka
B.	New Manglore Port	2.	Odisha
C.	Paradwip Port	3.	Maharashtra

Codes

	A	B	C		A	B	C
(a)	1	2	3	(b)	2	1	3
(c)	2	3	1	(d)	3	1	2

India: Human Resource (Population)

1 Mark Questions

1. The rank of India in terms of population among the countries of the world is ....
   (a) Fifth (b) First
   (c) Third (d) Second

2. Which among the following census years is also known as the Year of Demographic Divide?
   (a) 2001 (b) 2011 (c) 1921 (d) 1951

3. Uttar Pradesh has the largest share of Population of India, which of these has the second largest?
   (a) Bihar
   (b) Madhya Pradesh
   (c) Karnataka
   (d) Maharashtra

4. Which among the following states of India is the least populated among others?
   (a) Goa (b) Nagaland
   (c) Mizoram (d) Sikkim

5. Which of these states of India has the least density of population?
   (a) Arunachal Pradesh
   (b) Sikkim
   (c) Mizoram
   (d) Goa

6. Which of the following Union Territories of India has the highest population density among others?
   (a) Delhi (b) Ladakh
   (c) Puducherry (d) Lakshadweep

7. Which of these metropolitan areas has the largest population?
   (a) Delhi (b) Mumbai
   (c) Kolkata (d) Chennai

8. Which among the following states/UTs has the second highest literacy rate in India?
   (a) Arunachal Pradesh
   (b) Sikkim
   (c) Delhi
   (d) Ladakh

9. Which of these states has the highest female sex ratio in India?
   (a) Tamil Nadu (b) Andhra Pradesh
   (c) Kerala (d) Karnataka

10. The Dravidian group of people are inhabitants which of these regions of India?
    (a) North East Region
    (b) North West India
    (c) South India
    (d) Andaman and Nicobar Islands

11. Which of these states has the highest population of Schedule Tribes in India?
(a) Uttar Pradesh
(b) Mizoram
(c) Madhya Pradesh
(d) Rajasthan

12. Which of these states has the highest population of Schedule Castes?
(a) Bihar
(b) Andhra Pradesh
(c) Tamil Nadu
(d) Uttar Pradesh

13. The Largest population of Telugu Speakers resides in which of these states?
(a) Tamil Nadu   (b) Andhra Pradesh
(c) Kerala   (d) Karnataka

14. Hindi is the most spoken language in India, which is the second largest?
(a) Malyalam   (b) Punjabi
(c) Bengali   (d) Gujarati

15. Which among the following age groups contains the adolescent population?
(a) 5-15 years   (b) 10-19 years
(c) 25-45 years   (d) 18-50 years

2 Marks Questions

16. Which of these statements is true?
1. The Death rate has declined in India after Independence.
2. There has been a decrease in Life Expectancy at Birth in India after Independence.

Codes
(a) Only 1   (b) Only 2
(c) Both 1 and 2   (d) None of these

17. Match the following.

State		Feature
A. Haryana	1.	Highest Urbanisation
B. Bihar	2.	Lowest Literacy
C. Goa	3.	Lowest Sex Ratio

Codes

	A	B	C			A	B	C
(a)	3	1	2		(b)	2	1	3
(c)	3	2	1		(d)	1	3	2

18. Which among the following age groups is also known unproductive and dependent population?
1. 0-15 years
2. 15-59 years
3. 60-70 years

Codes
(a) Only 1 and 2   (b) Only 3
(c) Only 1 and 3   (d) Only 1

19. Which of the following statements is/are true?
1. The population in urban areas of India is more than the population of rural areas.
2. Delhi has the highest proportion of urban population in India.
3. Urbanisation is directly related with Industrialisation.

Codes
(a) Only 1 and 2   (b) Only 1 and 3
(c) Only 2 and 3   (d) All of these

20. Which among the following statements is/are correct?
1. Census of India is conducted in every 20 years.
2. The first digital census of India was conducted in 2011.
3. According to the previous Census, the male population of India is more than female population.

Codes
(a) Only 1   (b) Only 2
(c) Only 3   (d) All of these

Ecology and Environment

1 Mark Questions

1. Which of these scientists coined the term Biodiversity?
   (a) Walter G. Rosen
   (b) Charles Darwin
   (c) Ronald Fisher
   (d) William Harvey

2. Which among the following is an example of a Natural Ecosystem?
   (a) Zoo
   (b) Agricultural crop fields
   (c) Botanical Park
   (d) Teak Forests

3. Which among the following is an abiotic component of the Environment?
   (a) Plants   (b) Decomposers
   (c) Sunlight   (d) All of these

4. A series of complex interconnected foodchains is known as ....
   (a) Food Pyramid   (b) Ecotone
   (c) Succession   (d) Food Web

5. A Food Pyramid depicts which of the following?
   (a) Amount of energy transfer in a food chain
   (b) Trophic Levels of ecosystem
   (c) Productivity of Trophic Level
   (d) All of the above

6. Which among the following is an example of autotrophs?
   (a) Eagle   (b) Lion
   (c) Algae   (d) Humans

7. Which of the following is an example of Heterotrophs?
   (a) Bacteria
   (b) Plants
   (c) Green Algae
   (d) Fish

8. Which among the following is at the top of an Ecological Pyramid?
   (a) Decomposers
   (b) Primary Consumers
   (c) Heterotrophs
   (d) Tertiary Consumers

9. Bio decomposers can feed on dead remains of which of the following?
   (a) Producers
   (b) Primary Consumers
   (c) Tertiary Consumers
   (d) All of the above

10. What is the percentage of energy that is transferred from one trophic level to another?
    (a) Ninety   (b) Ten
    (c) Twenty Five   (d) Hundred

11. Which among the following is the main source of energy for water cycle?
(a) Wind Energy
(b) Tidal Energy
(c) Solar Energy
(d) Geothermal Energy

12. Conversion of natural gaseous nitrogen into ammonia is known as ....
(a) Ammonification
(b) Nitrogen Fixation
(c) De-nitrification
(d) Bacterial Fixation

13. Which among the following process is exactly opposite of Nitrogen Fixation?
(a) Ammonification
(b) Nitrification
(c) Assimilation
(d) De-nitrification

14. Which among the following organic molecules is made up of nitrogen?
(a) DNA
(b) RNA
(c) Lipids
(d) Both (a) and (b)

15. Which among the following processes adds carbon dioxide in the atmosphere?
(a) Photosynthesis
(b) Diffusion
(c) Respiration
(d) Condensation

16. Which among the following is a storehouse of carbon dioxide on the surface of Earth?
(a) Soil
(b) Trees and Plants
(c) Ocean Water
(d) All of these

17. Which among the following may decrease the harmful effects of Greenhouse Effect on Earth?
(a) Inter Cropping
(b) Afforestation
(c) Evapotranspiration
(d) Respiration

18. Which of the given options is an International Treaty that aims to protect the Ozone layer from depletion?
(a) Montreal Protocol
(b) Paris Agreement
(c) Ramsar Convention
(d) Kyoto Protocol

19. Which among the following is used to measure the extent of pollution in a water body?
(a) Dissolved Nitrogen
(b) Dissolved Oxygen
(c) Dissolved CO_2
(d) Chlorine

2 Marks Questions

20. Which of the following is/are the components of an ecosystem?

1. Microorganisms
2. Human beings
3. Animals
4. Soil

Codes
(a) Only 1, 2 and 3
(b) Only 1, 2 and 4
(c) Only 2, 3 and 4
(d) All of the above

21. Which among the following is/are the consequences of Global Warming and Climate Change?

1. Rise in Sea level
2. Increase in Global temperature
3. Rise in number of wetlands

Codes
(a) 1, 2 and 3
(b) Only 1 and 3
(c) Only 2 and 3
(d) Only 1 and 2

22. Consider the following stateements.

1. The herbivores occupy the second trophic level in a Food Chain.
2. The nutrients from dead animals are recycled by decomposers in a Food Chain.

Which of the statements given above is/are true?

Codes
(a) Only 1   (b) Only 2
(c) Both 1 and 2   (d) None of these

23. Which among the following steps can certainly help in reducing Ozone Depletion?

1. Reducing the use of Air Conditioners
2. Using electric Bikes and Cars
3. Reducing forest and tree cover

Codes
(a) Only 1 and 3   (b) 1, 2 and 3
(c) Only 1 and 2   (d) All of these

24. Which among the following compounds is/are responsible for Acid Rain?

1. Sulphur Dioxide
2. Carbon Dioxide
3. Nitrous Oxide

Codes
(a) Only 1 and 2   (b) Only 3
(c) Only 2   (d) Only 1 and 3

25. Match the following.

List I (Organism)		List II (Type)
A. Bacteria	1.	Heterotrophs
B. Birds	2.	Autotrophs
C. Yeast	3.	Saprophytes

Codes

	A	B	C			A	B	C
(a)	3	1	2		(b)	2	1	3
(c)	1	3	2		(d)	1	2	3

26. Consider the following statements.

1. The flow of energy in a food chain is unidirectional.
2. Harmful chemicals can enter the Human Food through the food chain.
3. Human beings are located at the top of the food chain.

Which of the statements given above is/are true?

Codes
(a) Only 1   (b) Only 1 and 2
(c) Only 1 and 3   (d) All of these

Chapter

18

Constitution

1 Mark Questions

1. The first attempt by Indian nationalists to write a Constitution for India resulted in making of which of these documents?
   (a) Government of India Act 1935
   (b) Nehru Report 1928
   (c) Karachi Resolution 1931
   (d) Desai Liaqat Pact

2. The Constitution of free India was adopted by which of these bodies?
   (a) The Parliament of India
   (b) The Parliament of Britain
   (c) The Governor General of India
   (d) The Constituent Assembly of India

3. The Constitution of India was adopted by the Constituent Assembly in which of these years?
   (a) 1947
   (b) 1949
   (c) 1950
   (d) 1951

4. Which of these personalities was the Chairman of the Drafting Committee of the Constituent Assembly?
   (a) Jawaharlal Nehru
   (b) B.N. Rau
   (c) Sardar Vallabbhai Patel
   (d) Dr. B.R. Ambedkar

5. Which of the following parts of the constitution describes India as a secular state?
   (a) Fundamental Rights
   (b) Directive Principles of State Policy
   (c) The Preamble   (d) Tenth Schedule

6. The term 'Socialist' was added to the Preamble through which of these amendments?
   (a) 103rd Amendment
   (b) 42nd Amendment
   (c) 1st Amendment
   (d) 100th Amendment

7. The Constitution of India makes provisions for which of the following type of governments in India?
   (a) Presidential form of government
   (b) Monarchical form of government
   (c) Parliamentary form of government
   (d) Democratic form of government

8. The Constitution of India provides which of the following type of Justices to the Indian citizen?
   (a) Social Justice
   (b) Economic Justice
   (c) Political Justice
   (d) All of the above

9. Which among the following is the lengthiest Written Constitution in the World?
   (a) American Constitution
   (b) Indian Constitution
   (c) German Constitution
   (d) Japanese Constitution

10. The ideas of Liberty, Equality and Fraternity in the Constitution have been derived from which of the following countries?
    (a) United States of America
    (b) France
    (c) Germany
    (d) United Kingdom

11. Which part of the Constitution of India deals with the matter of Citizenship?
    (a) Part I
    (b) Part X
    (c) Part II
    (d) Part III

12. The Constitution of India has been divided into how many parts?
    (a) Twenty-two
    (b) Ten
    (c) Thirty-Six
    (d) Fifteen

13. How many schedules are there in the Indian Constitution?
    (a) Five
    (b) Ten
    (c) Twenty
    (d) Twelve

14. Which of these type of emergencies cannot be declared according to provisions in the Constitution?
    (a) Financial Emergency
    (b) National Emergency
    (c) State Emergency
    (d) Natural Emergency

15. Which of the following type of emergencies has never been declared in India?
    (a) National Emergency
    (b) State Emergency
    (c) Financial Emergency
    (d) Both (a) and (c)

16. According to the Constitution, which of these has the power to declare war or peace with other nations?
    (a) The Defence Minister
    (b) The Chief of Indian Army
    (c) The President
    (d) The Vice President

17. Which of these schedules of Constitution gives details of subjects in Union, State and Concurrent List?
    (a) First Schedule   (b) Third Schedule
    (c) Seventh Schedule
    (d) Tenth Schedule

18. Which of these institutions can create a new state or alter boundaries of an existing state in India?
    (a) The Union Cabinet
    (b) The Supreme Court of India
    (c) The Parliament of India
    (d) The Rajya Sabha

19. Which of these is the official language of India according to the constitution?
    (a) Only English   (b) Only Urdu
    (c) Both English and Hindi
    (d) Only Hindi

20. According to the provisions of the Constitution, the Comptroller and Auditor General (CAG) is appointed by which of the following?
    (a) The Prime Minister of India
    (b) The President of India
    (c) The Finance Minister of India
    (d) The Vice President of India

2 Marks Questions

21. Consider the following statements.

1. The provisions of Indian Constitution is borrowed from various constitutions of the world.
2. The Constitution can be amended both by the Parliament and State Legislatures.

Which of the statements given above is/are true?

Codes

(a) Only 1   (b) Only 2
(c) Both 1 and 2   (d) None of these

22. Consider the following statements.

1. The Constitution of India has been amended only twice.
2. Any amendment to the Constitution has to pass through the Supreme Court.

Which of the statements given above is/are true?

Codes

(a) Only 1   (b) Only 2
(c) Both 1 and 2   (d) None of these

23. Consider the following statements.

1. According to the Constitution, India is a sovereign and secular country.
2. The real sovereign power is in the hands of the people.
3. The Indian government cannot discriminate among the people on the basis of religion.

Which of the statements given above is/are true?

Codes

(a) Only 1   (b) Only 3
(c) Only 1 and 3   (d) 1, 2 and 3

24. Consider the following statements.

1. The aims and objectives of the Constitution are mentioned in the Preamble.
2. India is a federal country where power is divided between Parliament and States.
3. The parliamentary form of government is borrowed from the Constitution of Britain.

Which of the statements given above is/are true?

Codes

(a) Only 1 and 2   (b) Only 1 and 3
(c) Only 3   (d) All of these

25. Match the following.

List I (Term in Constitution)	List II (Meaning)
A. Secular	1. Elected head of government
B. Liberty	2. Freedom to choose any religion
C. Republic	3. No unreasonable restrictions

Codes

	A	B	C			A	B	C
(a)	3	1	2		(b)	2	3	1
(c)	1	3	2		(d)	1	2	3

26. Which of the following pairs is correctly matched?

List I	List II
A. B. N Rau	1. Advisor to Constituent Assembly
B. Rajendra Prasad	2. President of Constituent Assembly
C. Mahatma Gandhi	3. Member of Constituent Assembly

Codes

(a) Only 1   (b) Only 2
(c) Only 3   (d) Only 1 and 2

Fundamental Rights/ Duties and DPSPs

1 Mark Questions

1. The Fundamental Rights have been adopted by India from which of these countries?
   (a) United Kingdom
   (b) United States of America
   (c) Russia
   (d) France

2. Which of these is not a fundamental right guaranteed by the constitution of India?
   (a) Right to Freedom of Speech
   (b) Right to Practise any Religion
   (c) Right to Property
   (d) Right to Constitutional Remedies

3. If a person is discriminated on the basis of religion, which of these fundamental rights is denied to him?
   (a) Right against Exploitation
   (b) Right to Freedom of Religion
   (c) Right to Life
   (d) Right to Equality

4. If the state violates the Fundamental Rights of a person, he/she can directly go to which of these courts?
   (a) Division Court   (b) Supreme Court
   (c) High Court   (d) Both (b) and (c)

5. The Right to Life is guaranteed under which article of the Constitution?
   (a) Article 19   (b) Article 21
   (c) Article 1   (d) Article 15

6. Which of these articles of the Constitution has provided the fundamental right against untouchability?
   (a) Article 21
   (b) Article 12
   (c) Article 17
   (d) Article 2

7. Which of these is not one of the six freedoms guaranteed by Article 19 of Fundamental Rights?
   (a) Freedom of association
   (b) Freedom of speech
   (c) Freedom of marrying
   (d) Freedom of trade

8. The Fundamental Rights of which of the following can be taken away by the Parliament if the need arises?
   (a) The MLAs
   (b) The Armed Forces
   (c) The Journalists
   (d) The Government Servants

9. Which of the following can impose restrictions upon the Fundamental Rights of an individual?
   (a) The Parliament
   (b) The Union Cabinet
   (c) The High Court
   (d) The President

10. Dr. B.R. Ambedkar described which of these as the Heart and Soul of the Constitution?
    (a) Right to Freedom of Speech and Expression
    (b) Right to Assemble and Protest Peaceably
    (c) Right against Untouchability
    (d) Right to Constitutional Remedies

11. Under which of the following emergencies, fundamental rights can be suspended?
    (a) President's Rule in a State
    (b) Financial Emergency
    (c) Natural Disasters
    (d) National Emergency

12. What are the reasonable restrictions on the fundamental rights mentioned in the Constitution?
    (a) Public Order
    (b) Public Morality
    (c) Security of the State
    (d) All of the above

13. Which of these fundamental rights protects the interests of the minorities?
    (a) Freedom to manage educational institutions
    (b) Freedom to protect language and script
    (c) Freedom to practise and propagate any religion
    (d) All of the above

14. Which among the following is a fundamental duty?
    (a) Duty to vote in every election
    (b) Duty to promote harmony and brotherhood
    (c) Duty to pay taxes regularly
    (d) Duty to respect elderly

15. Which among the following is not a fundamental duty?
    (a) To value rich heritage and composite culture of India
    (b) To respect the National Flag
    (c) To safeguard public property
    (d) To serve in the Indian Army

16. Which among the following is the latest fundamental duty to be added in the constitution?
    (a) To protect and improve natural environment
    (b) To defend the country and render national service
    (c) To develop scientific temper, humanism and spirit of enquiry
    (d) To provide educational opportunities to one's child between 6-14 years of age

17. Which among the following is a Gandhian Principle of the DPSPs?
    (a) Free and compulsory education for all
    (b) Promotion of cottage industries
    (c) Protecting monuments
    (d) Prevent concentration of wealth

2 Marks Questions

18. Which of these is true about the Fundamental Rights?

1. The fundamental rights are enforced by the Courts by the use of writs.
2. The chapter on Fundamental Rights were added through a constitutional amendment.

Codes
(a) Only 1   (b) Only 2
(c) Both 1 and 2   (d) None of these

19. The right to equality mentioned in the Constitution is enforced by which among the following provisions?

1. Right to freedom from exploitation
2. Equality before Law
3. Prohibition of discrimination

Codes
(a) Only 1   (b) Only 1 and 2
(c) Only 1 and 3   (d) All of these

20. Consider the following statements.

1. The Directive Principles are the ideas that the state should keep in mind while making laws.
2. Directive Principles are classified as Liberal, Socialist and Gandhian principles.
3. Directive Principles are enforceable in courts.

Which of the statements given above is/are true?

Codes
(a) Only 1   (b) Only 1 and 3
(c) 1, 2 and 3   (d) Only 1 and 2

21. Which among the following is correctly matched?

1.	Right to equal opportunities in public employment	Fundamental Right
2.	To promote cooperative societies	Fundamental Duty
3.	Strive for excellence in all spheres of life	Directive Principle

Codes
(a) Only 1   (b) Only 2
(c) Only 1 and 2   (d) Only 1 and 3

22. Which of the following is correctly matched?

	Article	**Right**
1.	Article 21	Right to Life
2.	Article 14	Right to Equality
3.	Article 25	Right to Freedom of Religion

Codes
(a) Only 2   (b) Only 3
(c) Only 1 and 3   (d) All of these

Chapter 20

Our Government

1 Mark Questions

1. Which of the following is the head of the government in India?
   (a) The President
   (b) The Prime Minister
   (c) The Home Minister
   (d) The Vice President

2. Which of the following ministers hold the highest position in the government?
   (a) Ministers of State
   (b) Ministers of State with Independent Charge
   (c) Cabinet Ministers
   (d) Deputy Ministers

3. The Parliament has the right to impeach which of the following?
   (a) Prime Minister
   (b) Defence Minister
   (c) President
   (d) Cabinet Ministers

4. Who among the following discharges the functions of the President during his absence?
   (a) Prime Minister
   (b) Solicitor General
   (c) Chief Justice of India
   (d) Vice President

5. What is the minimum age required to be elected as the Prime Minister of India?
   (a) 18 years   (b) 21 years
   (c) 35 years   (d) 25 years

6. To become the Prime Minister, a person has to be appointed as the member of which of the following?
   (a) Rajya Sabha
   (b) Lok Sabha
   (c) Any State Legislative Assembly
   (d) Either (a) or (b)

7. Who among the following chairs the proceedings of Lok Sabha?
   (a) The Prime Minister
   (b) The President
   (c) The Speaker
   (d) The Attorney General

8. During emergency, the tenure of Lok Sabha can be extended for a period of
   (a) 2 years   (b) 1 year
   (c) 6 months   (d) 1 month

9. How many members are appointed by the President in the Rajya Sabha?
   (a) Twelve   (b) Nine
   (c) Two   (d) Six

10. Which of the following is true about Upper House of Parliament?
(a) The maximum strength is 250 members.
(b) It cannot be dissolved.
(c) It represents the states of India.
(d) All of the above

11. Which among the following is the head of the government in a state?
(a) The Governor
(b) The Chief Minister
(c) The Solicitor General
(d) The President

12. Which of the following state has both an Upper House and a Lower House in its legislative assembly?
(a) Gujarat
(b) Sikkim
(c) Haryana
(d) Uttar Pradesh

13. The normal term of a State Legislative Assembly is ....
(a) 6 years
(b) 5 years
(c) 10 years
(d) 4 years

2 Marks Questions

14. Which of the following statements is/are true about the Lok Sabha?

1. The members of Lok Sabha are elected by direct elections.
2. The Prime Minister is the leader of the house in Lok Sabha.

Codes
(a) Only 1
(b) Only 2
(c) Both 1 and 2
(d) None of these

15. Which among the following statements is/are true?

1. The minimum age for voting in Elections is 21 years.
2. The elections to the Lok Sabha are held in every 6 years.
3. The Lok Sabha is automatically dissolved if the cabinet ministers resign.

Codes
(a) Only 1   (b) Only 3
(c) Only 1 and 3   (d) None of these

16. Which of the following is true about the Parliament of India?

1. The Parliament is organised into two houses.
2. The Rajya Sabha is the Lower House of the Parliament.
3. The Parliament can make laws for the governance of the country.

Codes
(a) Only 1   (b) Only 1 and 3
(c) Only 1 and 2   (d) All of these

17. Which among the following is/are correctly matched?

	Functionary	Appointed by
1.	Cabinet Ministers	The President
2.	The Lieutenant Governor	The Prime Minister
3.	The Chief Minister	Governor

Codes
(a) Only 1   (b) Only 1 and 2
(c) Only 1 and 3   (d) All of these

Our Judiciary

1 Mark Questions

1. The Supreme Court of Independent India was established in which year?
   (a) 1947   (b) 1950   (c) 1952   (d) 1961

2. The President appoints the Judges of Supreme court after consulting which among the following?
   (a) Prime Minister
   (b) Minister of Law
   (c) Chief Justice of India
   (d) Lieutenant Governor of Delhi

3. The President has the power to seek advisory opinion from which of the following courts?
   (a) High Court of Delhi
   (b) The Supreme Court
   (c) The Sessions Court
   (d) The Lok Adalats

4. The salaries and allowances of the judges of High Court can be altered by which of the following?
   (a) The Parliament
   (b) Delhi Legislative Assembly
   (c) The Rajya Sabha
   (d) Lieutenant Governor of Delhi

5. Which of the following was the first High Court in India?
   (a) Madras High Court
   (b) Delhi High Court
   (c) Calcutta High Court
   (d) Punjab and Haryana High Court

6. Which of the following State has a common High Court with a Union Territory of India?
   (a) Kerala
   (b) Madhya Pradesh
   (c) Uttar Pradesh   (d) Telangana

7. Which of the following high courts has the highest number of judges?
   (a) Bombay High Court
   (b) Madras High Court
   (c) Allahabad High Court
   (d) Calcutta High Court

8. The transfer of judges from one High Court to another High Court is done by which of the following?
   (a) Governor of the State
   (b) The President of India
   (c) The Attorney General of India
   (d) The Law Minister of India

9. Which of the following High Courts has separate benches at Panaji and Aurangabad?
   (a) Bombay High Court
   (b) Calcutta High Court
   (c) Gujarat High Court
   (d) Allahabad High Court

10. The Karnataka High Court is situated in which of the following cities?
(a) Mysore　　(b) Bengaluru
(c) Mangalore　　(d) Kolar

11. Which of the following system is used by the Judiciary in India for appointments and transfer of Judges in Supreme Court and High Courts?
(a) Cabinet system
(b) Collegium system
(c) Council system
(d) Nomination system

12. Which of the following courts has the power to punish individuals for contempt?
(a) Sessions Court　　(b) High Court
(c) Supreme Court　　(d) Both (b) and (c)

13. The judges in district courts are appointed by which of the following?
(a) The Governor
(b) The Chief Minister
(c) The Law minister in state
(d) The President

14. The system of Public Interest Litigation was started by which of the following?
(a) The Jammu and Kashmir High Court
(b) The Supreme Court
(c) The Delhi High Court
(d) The Parliament

15. The first Lok Adalat in India was organised by which of the following states?
(a) Tamil Nadu　　(b) Kerala
(c) Gujarat　　(d) Assam

2 Marks Questions

16. Which of the following is/are the powers of the Supreme Court?
1. Resolve dispute between a state and Central Government
2. Transfer of a case from one court to another
3. Review the judgements of a High Court

Codes
(a) Only 1　　(b) Only 2
(c) Only 1 and 2　　(d) All of these

17. Which among the following is matched correctly?

List I (High Court)	List II (Located in)
1. Gujarat high Court	Ahmedabad
2. Kerala High Court	Thiruvananthapuram
3. Uttarakhand High Court	Nainital

Codes
(a) Only 1 and 2
(b) Only 2 and 3
(c) Only 1 and 3
(d) All of the above

18. Consider the following statements.
1. The District courts have the power to give death sentence in criminal matters.
2. The judges of district courts are appointed by the High court of the state.

Which of the statements given above is/are true?

Codes
(a) Only 1
(b) Only 2
(c) Both 1 and 2
(d) None of the above

Panchayati Raj

1 Mark Questions

1. Which of the following committees recommended the implementation of Panchayati Raj system in India?
   (a) Punchi Commission
   (b) Butler Committee
   (c) Balwant Rai Mehta Committee
   (d) None of the above

2. Which of the following committees recommended a two tier Panchayati Raj in India?
   (a) Ashok Mehta Committee
   (b) L.M Singhvi Committee
   (c) GVK Committee
   (d) None of the above

3. Which was the first state to hold elections to the Panchayats after the constitutional implementation of Panchayati Raj System?
   (a) Odisha
   (b) Rajasthan
   (c) Madhya Pradesh
   (d) Gujarat

4. Rajasthan was the first to have Panchayati Raj system, which of these were the second?
   (a) Arunachal Pradesh
   (b) Andhra Pradesh
   (c) Jammu and Kashmir
   (d) Haryana

5. Which of these amendments to the Constitution gave constitutional status to Panchayati Raj institutions in India?
   (a) 100th Amendment
   (b) 73rd Amendment
   (c) 10th Amendment
   (d) 25th Amendment

6. Which of the following local bodies consists of all registered voters in electoral roll of the Panchayat?
   (a) Gram Panchayat
   (b) Panchayat Samiti
   (c) Gram Sabha
   (d) Zila Parishad

7. Which of the following is the highest institution in Panchayati Raj?
   (a) Gram Panchayat
   (b) Panchayat Samiti
   (c) Zilla Parishad
   (d) Mandal Parishad

8. Which of the following is a compulsory provision of the Panchayati Raj system in India?
(a) Giving power to Panchayats for levying taxes
(b) Fixed 5 years tenure
(c) Reservation for Women
(d) Both (b) and (c)

9. Which among the following bodies makes plans for development of panchayats and municipal areas?
(a) Planning Commission
(b) NITI Aayog
(c) District Planning Committee
(d) State Planning Commission

2 Marks Questions

10. Consider the following statements.
1. The distribution of finances to the local bodies is done by State Finance Commission.
2. The State Finance Commissioner is appointed by the Governor of the state.

Which of the following statements given above is/are true?

Codes
(a) Only 1   (b) Only 2
(c) Both 1 and 2   (d) None of these

11. Which among the following statements is/are correct?
1. The members of Gram Panchayat are directly elected by the people.
2. The members of Panchayat Samiti are elected for a period of 5 years.

Codes
(a) Only 1
(b) Only 2
(c) Both 1 and 2
(d) None of the above

12. Consider the following statements.
1. Gram Panchayat is the intermediate level in a three-tier Panchayat system.
2. The Panchayat Samiti acts as a link between Gram Panchayat and Zila Parishad.

Which of the following statements given above is/are correct?

Codes
(a) Only 1   (b) Only 2
(c) Both 1 and 2   (d) None of these

13. Which among the following is matched correctly?

	Type	Level
1.	Gram Panchayat	Block Level
2.	Mandal Parishad	District Level
3.	Panchayat Samiti	Block Level

Codes
(a) Only 1
(b) Only 2
(c) Only 3
(d) 1, 2 and 3

Indian Economy

1 Mark Questions

1. Which of the following Prime Ministers introduced the concept of Planning in India?
   (a) Morarji Desai
   (b) Jawaharlal Nehru
   (c) Manmohan Singh
   (d) Lal Bahadur Shastri

2. Which of the following Five Year Plans focused on Rapid Industrialisation?
   (a) Third Five Year Plan
   (b) First Five Year Plan
   (c) Second Five Year Plan
   (d) Sixth Five Year Plan

3. The Second Five Year Plan was based on which of the following models?
   (a) Harrod Domar Model
   (b) Nehru Mahalanobis Model
   (c) Gadgil Model
   (d) Sector Model

4. Which of the following Five Year Plans aimed at sustainable inclusive development?
   (a) First Five Year Plan
   (b) Twelfth Five Year Plan
   (c) Ninth Five Year Plan
   (d) Second Five Year Plan

5. The Planning Commission was replaced by NITI Aayog in which of the following year?
   (a) 2011   (b) 2015
   (c) 2020   (d) 2009

6. Which of the following sectors of economy is reserved for the Public Sector?
   (a) Hydroelectricity generation
   (b) Chemical Manufacturing
   (c) Atomic Energy
   (d) Education

7. The New Industrial Policy of 1991 contained which of the following features?
   (a) De reservation of Industrial Sectors
   (b) Introduction of Industrial Licencing
   (c) Allowing Foreign Investment Inflows
   (d) Both (a) and (c)

8. Which of the following sectors is the second largest employment provider in India after agriculture?
   (a) Computer Components
   (b) Textiles
   (c) Shipbuilding
   (d) Publishing

9. Automobile Manufacturing is included in which of the following sectors of Economy?
   (a) Primary Sector
   (b) Tertiary Sector
   (c) Secondary Sector
   (d) Quaternary Sector

10. In the foreign trade sector of Indian Economy, BoP stands for which of the following?
    (a) Balance out Product
    (b) Balance of Payments
    (c) Balance of Prices
    (d) Bond of Payments

11. A country's poverty line can be estimated in terms of PPP, the terms PPP stands for?
    (a) Purchasing Price Problems
    (b) Purchasing Power Parity
    (c) Purchasing Power of Products
    (d) Products Purchasing Problems

12. Which of the following sector of India's economy is the largest contributor to Foreign Direct Investment in India?
    (a) Automobile Industry
    (b) Chemicals and Fertilisers
    (c) Drugs and Pharmaceuticals
    (d) Service Sector

13. Which of the following is an example of Fast Moving Consumer Goods industry in India?
    (a) Packaged Food   (b) Automobiles
    (c) Air-conditioners (d) Mobile Phones

14. Which of the following is the largest public sector undertaking in India?
    (a) Indian Oil Corporation Ltd
    (b) State Bank of India
    (c) Indian Railways
    (d) Coal India Ltd

15. Which of the following is a direct tax?
    (a) Goods and Service Tax
    (b) Value Added Tax
    (c) Income Tax
    (d) Excise Duty

16. The Goods and Service Tax does not apply to which of the following products?
    (a) Milk   (b) Tea
    (c) Petroleum   (d) Steel Products

2 Marks Questions

17. Consider the following statements.
    1. GDP is the value of all goods and services produced in the country in one year.
    2. Increase in GDP leads to increasing happiness and mental health.

    Which of the statements given above is/are true?

    Codes
    (a) Only 1   (b) Only 2
    (c) Both 1 and 2   (d) None of these

18. Which of the following reduces productivity of labour in an economy?
    1. Inadequate sanitation
    2. Poor primary health services
    3. Low amount of nutrition

    Codes
    (a) Only 1 and 2
    (b) Only 1 and 3
    (c) Only 2 and 3
    (d) All of the above

19. Consider the following statements.

1. Make in India programme was started by the government to boost manufacturing sector growth.
2. The manufacturing sector is the largest contributor to the GDP of India.
3. Building and construction are included in the manufacturing sector of India.

Which of the statements given above is/are true?

Codes
(a) Only 1   (b) Only 3
(c) Only 1 and 3   (d) 1, 2 and 3

20. Consider the following statements.

1. Loans provided by Indian banking sector are supervised by the RBI.
2. Self Help Groups are formed to empower women and weaker sections.
3. Self Help Groups can provide loans to women at cheaper rates than informal loans.

Which of the given statements is/are true?

Codes
(a) Only 1   (b) Only 2
(c) Both 1 and 2   (d) All of these

21. Which of the following are correct forms of acronyms?

	List I (Term)	**List II** (Meaning)
1.	NDP	Net Domestic Product
2.	SEZ	Special Economic Zone
3.	BoT	Balance of Trade

Codes
(a) Only 1
(b) Only 2
(c) Only 1 and 2
(d) All of the above

22. Which of the following is matched correctly?

1.	Liberalisation	Removing trade restrictions
2.	Privatisation	Transfer of ownership from private sector to public sector
3.	Globalisation	Integrating home economy with foreign economies

Codes
(a) Only 1
(b) Only 2
(c) Only 1 and 3
(d) Only 2 and 3

Poverty and Employment

1 Mark Questions

1. Which of the following committees is associated with Poverty Estimation?
   (a) Kasturirangan Committee
   (b) Rangarajan Committee
   (c) Balwant Rai Mehta Committee
   (d) All of the above

2. Which of the following committees suggested a uniform poverty line across Rural and Urban areas of India?
   (a) Alagh Committee
   (b) Tendulkar Committee
   (c) Lakdawala Committee
   (d) Rangarajan Committee

3. Which of the following types of poverty occurs due to a sudden adverse event?
   (a) Generational Poverty
   (b) Situational Poverty
   (c) Relative Poverty
   (d) Absolute Poverty

4. The absence of which of the following conditions in rural areas can lead to increase in Rural Poverty?
   (a) Agricultural land
   (b) Infrastructure
   (c) Health and education
   (d) All of the above

5. Which of the following states has the largest number of poor people living Below Poverty Line?
   (a) Arunachal Pradesh
   (b) Andhra Pradesh
   (c) Jammu and Kashmir
   (d) Chhattisgarh

6. The first poverty alleviation program in India was started in which of the following years?
   (a) 1991   (b) 1950   (c) 1978   (d) 2001

7. The Tendulkar Committee estimated the poverty line on the basis of which among the following?
   (a) Calorie Intake
   (b) Consumption Expenditure
   (c) Access to Education
   (d) Access to Food

8. If there is a mismatch between supply of jobs and skills of available workers in the market, it signifies which of the following?
   (a) Disguised Unemployment
   (b) Frictional Unemployment
   (c) Underemployment
   (d) Structural Unemployment

9. Which of the following conditions occur when people are unemployed for short durations of time?
(a) Frictional Unemployment
(b) Under Employment
(c) Disguised Unemployment
(d) Chronic Unemployment

10. The agricultural sector of India witnesses which of the following types of unemployment?
(a) Seasonal Unemployment
(b) Disguised Unemployment
(c) Under Employment
(d) Both (a) and (b)

11. If an Engineer is working as a salesman for a small firm, it characterises which of the following condition?
(a) Under Employment
(b) Voluntary Unemployment
(c) Open Unemployment
(d) Cyclical Unemployment

12. Under the Mahatma Gandhi National Rural Employment scheme, what proportion of total employees must be women?
(a) Two-third   (b) One-third
(c) One-sixth   (d) One-tenth

2 Marks Questions

13. Consider the following statements.
1. Unemployment data is collected in India by the Central Statistical Office.
2. The labour force participation of women is highest in India.

Which of the statements given above is/are true?

Codes
(a) Only 1   (b) Only 2
(c) Both 1 and 2   (d) None of these

14. Consider the following statements.
1. Agriculture sector is the largest employer of rural women in India.
2. Manufacturing sector is the largest employer of urban women in India.

Which of the statements given above is/are true?

Codes
(a) Only 1
(b) Only 2
(c) Both 1 and 2
(d) None of the above

15. Which of the following are anti-poverty schemes started by the Government in India?
1. Food for Work Program
2. Antyodaya Scheme
3. National Rural Livelihood Mission
4. Sarva Shiksha Abhiyan

Codes
(a) Only 1 and 3   (b) Only 2, 3 and 4
(c) Only 1, 3 and 4   (d) All of these

16. Consider the following statements.
1. Construction sector is the largest employment provider in the unorganised sector.
2. Indian railways is the largest public sector employer in India.

Which of the statements given above is/are true?

Codes
(a) Only 1   (b) Only 2
(c) Both 1 and 2   (d) None of these

Money and Banking

1 Mark Questions

1. Currency printing press is located at which of the following places in India?
(a) Mumbai   (b) Nashik
(c) Delhi   (d) Bilaspur

2. Which of the following currency notes does not bear the signature of RBI Governor?
(a) ₹ 100   (b) ₹ 20
(c) ₹ 1   (d) ₹ 500

3. Which of the following currency notes in India is issued by the Finance Ministry?
(a) ₹ 2,000   (b) ₹ 500
(c) ₹ 1   (d) ₹ 10

4. Which among the following coins is made up of Stainless steel?
(a) ₹ 5   (b) ₹ 2
(c) ₹ 20   (d) ₹ 10

5. Hundred Rupee currency note in India has which of the following motifs?
(a) Rani ki Vav
(b) Mangalyan
(c) Red Fort
(d) Sanchi Stupa

6. The Indian Currency note has the amount written in a total of how many languages?
(a) 20 languages   (b) 17 languages
(c) 22 languages   (d) 10 languages

7. Which of the following was the first coin mint of India?
(a) Hyderabad Mint
(b) Noida Mint
(c) Calcutta Mint
(d) Bombay Mint

8. Which among the following has the power to impose fines upon commercial banks in India?
(a) Small Industries Development Bank
(b) Reserve Bank of India
(c) State Bank of India
(d) Punjab National Bank

9. The Governor of Reserve Bank of India is selected by which of the following?
(a) The Cabinet
(b) The President
(c) The Deputy Governors
(d) Minister of Corporate Affairs

10. Bank Nationalisation was carried out by which of the following Prime Ministers for the first time?
(a) Indira Gandhi
(b) Rajiv Gandhi
(c) Jawahar Lal Nehru
(d) Atal Bihari Vajpayee

11. Which of the following is the largest Public Sector Bank in India?
(a) Punjab National Bank
(b) State Bank of India
(c) Canara Bank
(d) Union Bank of India

12. The headquarters of Punjab National Bank is located in which of the following cities?
(a) New Delhi   (b) Mohali
(c) Jhajjhar   (d) Amritsar

13. In the banking sector, the term CRR stands for which of the following?
(a) Collateral Rising Ratio
(b) Cash Reserve Ratio
(c) Capital Regulation Ratio
(d) Cash Regulation Reserves

2 Marks Questions

14. Which of the following is correctly matched?

	Currency Note	Motif
1.	₹ 10	Konark Temple
2.	₹ 20	Ellora Cave
3.	₹ 50	Red Fort

Codes
(a) Only 1 and 2   (b) Only 2 and 3
(c) Only 3   (d) None of these

15. Which of the following functions are performed by the Reserve Bank of India?
1. Credit Control of Economy
2. Banker of the Government
3. Custodian of Foreign Reserves

Codes
(a) Only 1 and 3   (b) Only 2 and 3
(c) Only 1 and 2   (d) All of these

16. Which of the following statements is/are correct?
1. Rise in inflation reduces the purchasing power of money.
2. Indian currency notes are a form of Token Money.

Codes
(a) Only 1   (b) Only 2
(c) Both 1 and 2   (d) None of these

17. Which of the following type of banks were started for Financial Inclusion in India?
1. Payment Banks
2. Small Finance Banks
3. Regional Rural Banks

Codes
(a) Only 2 and 3   (b) Only 1 and 3
(c) Only 1 and 2   (d) All of these

Chapter 26

General Science

1 Mark Questions

1. What is the to and fro motion of a body called?
   (a) Rotatory Motion
   (b) Rectilinear Motion
   (c) Oscillatory Motion
   (d) Translatory Motion

2. The launch of a rocket and its fall after burn out depicts which of the following type of motion?
   (a) Linear Motion
   (b) Circular Motion
   (c) Projectile Motion
   (d) Circulatory Motion

3. The momentum of a body can be calculated by which of the following?
   (a) Mass × acceleration
   (b) Mass × velocity
   (c) Force × velocity
   (d) Speed × Force

4. Weight of an object changes from place to place because of which of the following?
   (a) Acceleration (b) Momentum
   (c) Gravity (d) Force

5. The energy possessed by a body due to its fixed position is known as ....
   (a) Kinetic Energy
   (b) Potential Energy
   (c) Heat Energy
   (d) Electrical Energy

6. Which of the following is the most elastic material?
   (a) Glass (b) Steel
   (c) Gold (d) Quartz

7. Pressure can be measured in which of the following units?
   (a) Ampere
   (b) Candela
   (c) Pascal
   (d) Mole

8. Bleeding in nose may occur when people move to higher altitude areas, this is because of which of the following phenomenon?
   (a) Gravity
   (b) Momentum
   (c) Atmospheric Pressure
   (d) Buoyancy

9. Which of the following is the internal force of friction in liquids?
   (a) Density   (b) Viscosity
   (c) Resonance   (d) Reflectance

10. The speed of a sound wave will be fastest in which of the following mediums?
    (a) Air   (b) Wooden Table
    (c) Vacuum   (d) Water

11. Concave mirrors can be used in which of the following?
    (a) Vehicle headlights
    (b) Rear view mirrors
    (c) Sharp turns on road
    (d) Magnifying glass

12. Stars appear to twinkle because of which of the following phenomenon?
    (a) Reflection
    (b) Refraction
    (c) Diffraction
    (d) Scattering

13. If a beam of white light is directed towards a prism, the least deviation will occur in which of the following colour beams?
    (a) Violet   (b) Blue
    (c) Green   (d) Red

14. Which of the following can act as an insulator to electric current?
    (a) Copper   (b) Gold
    (c) Mica   (d) Iron

15. Which of the following electromagnetic waves has the highest frequency?
    (a) Radio waves
    (b) X-rays
    (c) Infrared waves
    (d) Ultraviolet waves

16. The filament of an electric bulb is made from which of the following elements?
    (a) Iron   (b) Copper
    (c) Tungsten   (d) Radium

17. Which of the following is a ferromagnetic substance?
    (a) Iron   (b) Cobalt
    (c) Nickel   (d) All of these

18. Dry ice is a solid form of which of the following substances?
    (a) Oxygen   (b) Nitrogen
    (c) Carbon Dioxide   (d) Sulphur

19. Which of the following is an organic compound?
    (a) Salt   (b) Washing Soda
    (c) Lipid   (d) Marble

20. Which among the following conducted the gold foil experiment to determine the structure of atoms?
    (a) Neil Bohr   (b) John Dalton
    (c) E. Rutherford   (d) D. Mendeleev

21. Which of the following is a Lanthanoid in the Periodic Table?
    (a) Germanium   (b) Cadmium
    (c) Tin   (d) Cerium

22. Sour Milk contains which of the following acids?
    (a) Acetic Acid   (b) Maleic Acid
    (c) Tarteric Acid   (d) Lactic Acid

23. Which of the following acids is used in a Lead Acid battery?
    (a) Hydrochloric Acid
    (b) Sulphuric Acid
    (c) Nitric Acid
    (d) Carbonic Acid

24. Which among the following substances can be used for purification of water?
    (a) Sodium Benzoate
    (b) Alum
    (c) Vinegar
    (d) Both (b) and (c)

25. Fuse wires in electric circuits are made up of which of the following alloys?
    (a) Lead and Tin
    (b) Nickel and Chromium
    (c) Copper and Nickel
    (d) Iron and Tin

26. Which among the following is an exothermic process?
    (a) Combustion
    (b) Respiration
    (c) Setting of Cement
    (d) All of the above

27. Which of the following is a unicellular organism?
    (a) Fishes   (b) Bacteria
    (c) Human Beings   (d) Reptiles

28. Anaemia can be caused by deficiency of which of the following?
    (a) Flourine   (b) Iron
    (c) Zinc   (d) Selenium

29. Deficiency of Vitamin A can cause which of the following disease?
    (a) Beri-Beri   (b) Rickets
    (c) Scurvy   (d) Night Blindness

30. Which of the following is the smallest gland in human body?
    (a) Pancreas
    (b) Pineal Gland
    (c) Hypothalamus
    (d) Pituitary Gland

31. Which of the following is the carrier of genetic information in humans?
    (a) Nucleus   (b) Chloroplast
    (c) Chromosomes   (d) Lysosome

32. Which of the following is a reptile?
    (a) Bat   (b) Elephant
    (c) Mice   (d) Crocodile

33. Red Blood Cells are formed in which of the following?
    (a) Hypothalamus   (b) Bone Marrow
    (c) Liver   (d) Ligament

34. Which of the following Blood Cells protects the body from diseases?
    (a) Red Blood Cells
    (b) Leucocytes
    (c) Platelets
    (d) Thrombocytes

35. Sphygmomanometer is used to measure which of the following?
    (a) Blood Pressure   (b) Blood Sugar
    (c) Heartbeat   (d) Pulse

36. Which of the following part of brain is used for thinking?
    (a) Cerebrum   (b) Hypothalamus
    (c) Cerebellum   (d) Medulla

37. Which of the following organic compounds is used to regulate metabolism in the body?
    (a) Fats   (b) Vitamins
    (c) Protein   (d) All of these

38. Hepatitis affects which of the following organs?
    (a) Liver   (b) Eyes
    (c) Pancreas   (d) Kidney

2 Marks Questions

39. Which of the following statements is/are correct?

   1. The least dense metal is Lithium.

   2. Silver is the best conductor of electricity.

   3. Gold is a Nobel metal

Codes

(a) Only 1   (b) Only 2 and 3

(c) Only 1 and 3   (d) All of these

40. Which of the following is true regarding gravity?

   1. The value of gravity is maximum at the poles.

   2. Value of gravity decreases with height and depth from the surface.

   3. The acceleration due to gravity does not depend on shape and size of the body.

Codes

(a) Only 1 and 2   (b) Only 1 and 3

(c) Only 1   (d) Only 2 and 3

41. Which of the following is/are uses of Convex mirror?

   1. Sunglasses

   2. Rear View Mirrors

   3. Shaving Glass

   4. Search Light

Codes

(a) Only 1, 2 and 3

(b) Only 1 and 2

(c) Only 1, 3 and 4

(d) Only 1, 2 and 4

42. Which of the following is matched correctly?

	Field	Study of
1.	Dermatology	Study of Skin
2.	Cytology	Study of Cells
3.	Phycology	Study of Algae

Codes

(a) Only 1 and 3   (b) Only 1 and 2

(c) Only 2 and 3   (d) All of these

43. Match the following.

	List I (Quantity)		List II (Unit)
A.	Work	1.	Joule
B.	Power	2.	Watt
C.	Current	3.	Ampere

Codes

	A	B	C			A	B	C
(a)	2	3	1		(b)	3	1	2
(c)	3	2	1		(d)	1	2	3

Science and Technology

1 Mark Questions

1. The first generation of computers were made from which of the following?
   (a) Transistors
   (b) Vacuum Tubes
   (c) Microprocessors
   (d) Integrated Circuits

2. Which of the following was the first operating system?
   (a) Windows
   (b) MS DOS
   (c) Macintosh
   (d) GMOS

3. Which of the following is a type of secondary memory?
   (a) Random Access Memory
   (b) Read Only Memory
   (c) Hard Disk memory
   (d) Both (a) and (b)

4. Which of the following is an input device?
   (a) Visual Display Unit
   (b) Plotter
   (c) Optical Mark Reader
   (d) LED Monitor

5. Which of the following device is used to link different computer systems to the internet?
   (a) BIOS (b) Modem (c) UNIX (d) Linux

6. Which of the following is not an operating system?
   (a) Ubuntu   (b) Mac OS
   (c) Java   (d) Android

7. Which of the following systems can be used to connect computers to each other in an office building?
   (a) Local Area Network
   (b) Wide Area Network
   (c) Metropolitan Area Network
   d) Personal Area Network

8. Brahmos Supersonic ballistic missile has been built with collaboration of which of the following countries?
   (a) USA   (b) Mongolia
   (c) Russia   (d) China

9. Which of the following is an anti-tank missile?
   (a) Agni   (b) Nag
   (c) Prithvi   (d) Trishul

10. The headquarters of Defence Research and Development Organisation is located in which city?
(a) Mumbai
(b) New Delhi
(c) Chennai
(d) Hyderabad

11. Where is the center for DNA fingerprinting and diagnostics is located?
(a) Gurugram
(b) Hyderabad
(c) Chennai
(d) Pune

12. In a thermal power plant which energy gets converted into which form of energy?
(a) Mechanical energy to chemical energy
(b) Heat energy to electrical energy
(c) Chemical energy to solar energy
(d) Mechanical energy to electrical energy

13. Abdul Kalam Island, used for launching satellites in space, is located in which of the following states?
(a) West Bengal
(b) Odisha
(c) Andhra Pradesh
(d) Tamil Nadu

14. Which of the following is an Indian research centre stationed in Antarctica?
(a) Dakshin Gangotri
(b) Bharati
(c) Maitri
(d) All of these

15. Which among the following is the first privately funded satellite of India?
(a) HySYS
(b) Exseed Sat
(c) Kalam Sat
(d) HAMSAT

16. Which of the following was the second satellite launched by India?
(a) Bhaskara
(b) Rohini
(c) APPLE
(d) Swayam

17. Which of the following is India's first Earth Observatory?
(a) INSAT
(b) ASTROSAT
(c) GSLV
(d) GAGAN

18. The ADITYA mission of ISRO is for studying the outer surface of which of the following objects?
(a) Moon
(b) Sun
(c) Mars
(d) Jupiter

2 Marks Questions

19. Consider the following statements regarding stem cells.

1. Stem cells can increase their number by cell division.
2. They serve as a repair system for the body and can even be preserved.

Which of the following statements is/are true?

Codes
(a) Only 1
(b) Only 2
(c) Both 1 and 2
(d) None of the above

20. Match the following.

List I (Windows Shortcut)	List II (Use)
A. Ctrl + Y	1. Open start
B. Ctrl + Esc	2. Redo last action
C. Alt + F4	3. Close current program

Codes

	A	B	C			A	B	C
(a)	1	2	3		(b)	3	1	2
(c)	2	1	3		(d)	3	2	1

21. Consider the following statements.

1. The first generation computers produced large amount of heat.
2. The second generation computers were based on use of transistors.
3. Third generation computers used Integrated circuits.

Which of the statements given above is/are true?

Codes
(a) Only 1 and 2   (b) Only 2 and 3
(c) Only 1 and 3   (d) All of these

22. Consider the following statements.

1. The first aircraft carrier of India was INS Vikrant.
2. Rafale Fighter jet has been bought by India from Germany.
3. The Sukhoi fighter jet has been made with assistance from Russia.

Which of the statements given above is/are true?

Codes
(a) Only 1 and 2
(b) Only 1 and 3
(c) Only 1
(d) All of the above

23. Which of the following is matched correctly?

List I (Satellite)		List II (Purpose)
A. INSAT	1.	Communication
B. CARTOSAT	2.	Earth Observation
C. IRNSS	3.	Navigation

Codes
(a) Only 1 and 2
(b) Only 2 and 3
(c) Only 1 and 3
(d) All of the above

General Knowledge

1 Mark Questions

1. Who among the following was the first person to draw the map of Earth?
   (a) Anaximander
   (b) Marco Polo
   (c) W.K Roentgen
   (d) Robert Peary

2. Who among the following became the first female Prime Minister in the world?
   (a) Indira Gandhi
   (b) S. Bandaranaike
   (c) Golda Meir
   (d) Benazir Bhutto

3. Which of the following was the first women Governor of an Indian state?
   (a) Pratibha Patil
   (b) Vijaya Lakshmi Pandit
   (c) Sarojini Naidu
   (d) Sheila Dixit

4. Who was the first woman in the world who went to Space?
   (a) Kalpan Chawla
   (b) Helena Sharman
   (c) Valentina Tereshkova
   (d) Chiaki Mukai

5. Which of these was the first space shuttle in the world?
   (a) Discovery
   (b) Challenger
   (c) Columbia
   (d) Atlantis

6. Which of the following was the first country to successfully launch a mission to study Mars?
   (a) USA
   (b) China
   (c) Russia
   (d) Germany

7. Which of these country was the first to launch a competition for recruiting civil servants?
   (a) India
   (b) Great Britain
   (c) China
   (d) USA

8. Which of the following was the first nuclear reactor of Asia?
   (a) Apsara
   (b) Rohini
   (c) Aryabhatta
   (d) Nakshatra

9. The first nuclear test of India was code named as ....
   (a) Laughing Krishna
   (b) Operation Shakti
   (c) Smiling Buddha
   (d) Shakti Pradarshan

10. The first fighter jet of India was developed by which of the following?
    (a) Defence Research Development Organisation
    (b) Indian Space Research Organisation
    (c) Hindustan Aeronautics Ltd
    (d) Indian Rotorcraft Ltd

11. Which of the following was the longest serving President of India?
    (a) APJ Abdul Kalam
    (b) Fakhruddin Ali Ahmad
    (c) Rajendra Prasad
    (d) Pranav Mukharjee

12. Which of the following is the longest artificial canal in the world?
    (a) Indira Gandhi Canal
    (b) Hangzhou Grand Canal
    (c) Panama Canal
    (d) Eurasia Canal

13. Which of the following is the largest gateway in the world?
    (a) India Gate   (b) Brandenburg Gate
    (c) Buland Darwaza (d) Rumi Darwaza

14. Which of the following is the longest Metro subway system in the world?
    (a) Delhi metro
    (b) Seoul Metro
    (c) Shanghai Metro
    (d) New York Metro

15. Which of the following is the largest capital city of world in term of population?
    (a) Moscow   (b) Beijing
    (c) Jakarta   (d) New York

16. Which of the following is the largest spoken language of the world?
    (a) Hindi   (b) English
    (c) German   (d) Russian

17. Which of following is the largest peninsula of the world?
    (a) Yucatan Peninsula
    (b) Arabian Peninsula
    (c) Indo China Peninula
    (d) Alaska Peninsula

18. Which of the following is the largest river basin?
    (a) Ganga basin
    (b) Amazon basin
    (c) Nile basin
    (d) Yangtze basin

19. Which of the following is the largest cold desert of the world?
    (a) Gobi Desert
    (b) Antarctica Desert
    (c) Patagonia Desert
    (d) Takla Makan Desert

20. Largest diamond mine of the world is located in which of the following countries?
    (a) China   (b) Australia
    (c) Russia   (d) India

21. Which of the following is the world's largest international border?
    (a) India-China Border
    (b) USA-Canada Border
    (c) USA-Mexico Border
    (d) Argentina-Chile Border

22. Which of the following is the capital of Turkey?
    (a) Abu Dhabi   (b) Ankara
    (c) Damascus   (d) Amman

23. Which of the following is the Capital of Switzerland?
    (a) Zurich   (b) Bern
    (c) Geneva   (d) Basel

24. The currency of Italy is ....
    (a) Yen   (b) Won
    (c) Euro   (d) Pound

25. The currency of Bangladesh is ....
    (a) Taka   (b) Peso
    (c) Koruna   (d) Dinar

26. Which of the following is the currency of Russia?
    (a) Ruble (b) Leki (c) Peso (d) Euro

27. 'Dogri' is generally spoken in which of the following states?
    (a) Himachal Pradesh and Jammu
    (b) Bihar and Rajasthan
    (c) Andhra Pradesh
    (d) Tamil Nadu and Goa

28. Which of the following is the largest state in North-East India?
    (a) Assam
    (b) Arunachal Pradesh
    (c) Nagaland
    (d) Tripura

29. Which of the following is the smallest Union Territory of India in terms of area?
    (a) Andaman and Nicobar
    (b) Delhi
    (c) Lakshadweep
    (d) Ladakh

30. The state of Uttar Pradesh shares its border with which of the following countries?
    (a) China   (b) Pakistan
    (c) Myanmar   (d) Nepal

31. Which of these is the capital of Tripura?
    (a) Agartala
    (b) Gangtok
    (c) Aizwal
    (d) Shillong

32. Name the National game of United States of America?
    (a) Water Polo   (b) Rugby
    (c) Polo   (d) Baseball

33. The first ever Asian games were held in which of the following cities?
    (a) Seoul   (b) Beijing
    (c) New Delhi   (d) Tokyo

34. Which of the following Tennis Grand Slam is played in Clay court?
    (a) Australian Open
    (b) French Open
    (c) US Open
    (d) Wimbeldon

35. Which of the following is the first Indian Woman to win a medal in Paralympic Games?
    (a) Hima Das   (b) Dipa Karmakar
    (c) Deepika Kumari   (d) Deepa Malik

36. Ryder Cup is associated with which of the following sports?
    (a) Football   (b) Hockey
    (c) Golf   (d) Javelin Throw

37. Headquarters of International Cricket Council (ICC) is located in which country?
    (a) Dubai (UAE)   (b) New York (USA)
    (c) London (UK)   (d) Delhi (India)

38. The Booker Prize is awarded in which of the following fields?
    (a) Medicine   (b) Literature
    (c) Sports   (d) Social Service

39. Who among the following was the first Indian to win a Nobel Prize?
    (a) Hargobind Khorana
    (b) Dr. Homi Bhabha
    (c) Rabindra Nath Tagore
    (d) C.V. Raman

40. Ramon Magsaysay Award is an annual award, it is given all the fields except one mentioned below.

(a) Government Service

(b) Science Research

(c) Community Leadership

(d) Peace and International Understanding

41. Who among the following was the first Indian to win Nobel Prize in field of Economics?

(a) Amartya Sen

(b) Raghuram Rajan

(c) Manmohan Singh

(d) Abhijit Banerjee

2 Marks Questions

42. Match the following.

Country		Capital
A. Netherlands	1.	Berlin
B. Greece	2.	Amsterdam
C. Germany	3.	Athens

Codes

	A	B	C
(a)	1	2	3
(b)	2	3	1
(c)	3	1	2
(d)	3	2	1

43. Which of the following is matched correctly?

	Country	Nicknamed as
1.	South Africa	The rainbow nation
2.	Russia	The land of rising Sun
3.	Finland	Land of thousand lakes

Codes

(a) Only 1 and 2

(b) Only 2 and 3

(c) Only 1 and 3

(d) All of the above

44. Which of the following is correctly matched?

	Ministers	Name
1.	First Education Minister of India	Maulana Abul Kalam Azad
2.	First Law Minister of India	B. R. Ambedkar
3.	First Health Minister	Rajkumari Amrit Kaur

Codes

(a) 1, 2 and 3

(b) Only 1 and 2

(c) Only 2 and 3

(d) All of these

45. Match the following.

	City	Known as
A.	Allepy	1. City of Lakes
B.	Mumbai	2. Queen of Deccan
C.	Udaipur	3. Financial Capital of India
D.	Pune	4. Venice of India

Codes

	A	B	C	D			A	B	C	D
(a)	4	1	2	3		(b)	4	3	1	2
(c)	3	2	1	4		(d)	3	4	2	1

PRACTICE
SETS
1-2

PRACTICE SET 01

1 Mark Questions

1. Who was the founder of the Yoga Philosophy?
   (a) Gautama (b) Jaimini
   (c) Patanjali (d) Kapila

2. Gautama Buddha attained enlightenment at which of the following places?
   (a) Lumbini (b) Taxila
   (c) Bodh Gaya (d) Sarnath

3. Who among the following constructed the Tughlaqabad Fort?
   (a) Muhammad Bin Tughlaq
   (b) Ghiyasudin Tughlaq
   (c) Firoz Shah Tughlaq
   (d) Nassirudin Tughlaq

4. The Subsidiary alliance system was proposed by which among the following?
   (a) Lord Dalhousie
   (b) Lord Wellesley
   (c) Warren Hastings
   (d) Lord Curzon

5. Which of the following National leaders was also known as 'Patriot of Patriots'?
   (a) Mahatma Gandhi
   (b) Subhash Chandra Bose
   (c) Jawahar Lal Nehru
   (d) Bhagat Singh

6. Which of the following countries is associated with Nile Civilisation?
   (a) Turkey (b) Brazil
   (c) Egypt (d) Italy

7. Which among the following was a dictator of France?
   (a) Benito Mussolini
   (b) Napoleon Bonaparte
   (c) Robert Mugabe
   (d) Fidel Castro

8. Which of the following layers of atmosphere makes radio communication possible on Earth?
   (a) Mesosphere (b) Ionosphere
   (c) Exosphere (d) Troposphere

9. Which of the following layers of Earth is also known as Ni-Fe?
   (a) Mantle (b) Core
   (c) Crust (d) Troposphere

10. Which of the following rivers does not originate from the Himalayan region?
    (a) Brahmaputra (b) Alaknanda
    (c) Indus (d) Godavari

11. Which of these soils is found majorly in the Deccan Traps of India?
    (a) Alluvial Soil
    (b) Black Soil
    (c) Laterite Soil
    (d) Yellow Soil

12. Which of the following is the oldest Dam in India?
    (a) Nagarjunasagar Dam
    (b) Mettur Dam
    (c) Kallanai Dam
    (d) Tehri Dam

13. Which of the following is the first Atomic Power plant of India?
    (a) Naraura Atomic Power Plant
    (b) Kaiga Atomic Plant
    (c) Tarapur Atomic Plant
    (d) Madras Atomic Power Plant

14. Diamond Mines are found in which of the following regions of India?
    (a) Talcher   (b) Panna
    (c) Raniganj   (d) Gua

15. Which of the following is a plantation crop in India?
    (a) Coconut   (b) Cashew
    (c) Tea   (d) All of these

16. The Kharif Crops are sown in which of the following months in India?
    (a) November   (b) March
    (c) July   (d) September

17. Durgapur Steel Plant was setup with assistance from ....
    (a) United States   (b) United Kingdom
    (c) Russia   (d) Germany

18. Which of the following cities is also known as Manchester of India for its flourishing Cotton Textile industry?
    (a) Mumbai   (b) Surat
    (c) Ahmedabad   (d) Kolkata

19. Which of the following was the first railway zone of India?
    (a) Eastern Railway
    (b) Southern Railway
    (c) Western Railway
    (d) Northern Railway

20. The Grand Trunk Road connects which of the following cities of India?
    (a) Mumbai and Chennai
    (b) Amritsar and Kolkata
    (c) Srinagar and Thiruvananthapuram
    (d) Surat to Silchar

21. The Santhal and Munda tribe belong to which of the following states of India?
    (a) Madhya Pradesh (b) Chhattisgarh
    (c) Jharkhand   (d) Andhra Pradesh

22. The Valley of Flower National Park is located in between which of the following mountain range?
    (a) Aravalli
    (b) Purvanchal
    (c) Western Himalayas
    (d) Nilgiris

23. Decomposition of dead matter is carried out in presence of which of the following gases?
    (a) Nitrogen   (b) Carbon Dioxide
    (c) Oxygen   (d) Argon

24. The provision of Single citizenship has been taken from which of the following Constitutions?
    (a) United Kingdom (b) Ireland
    (c) USA   (d) Russia

25. The Constituent Assembly of India was setup under the framework of which of the following schemes?
    (a) Cripp's Mission Plan
    (b) Cabinet Mission Plan
    (c) Mountbatten Plan
    (d) Simon Commission

26. Which of the following article of the Constitution has abolished untouchability?
    (a) Article 14   (b) Article 15
    (c) Article 19   (d) Article 17

27. Which of the following is a fundamental duty mentioned in the Constitution?
    (a) To save and preserve water
    (b) To give up practises derogatory to dignity of women
    (c) To work hard and become great
    (d) To pay taxes on time

28. Which of the following states elects the highest number of members in Lok Sabha?
    (a) Madhya Pradesh (b) Tamil Nadu
    (c) Andhra Pradesh (d) Uttar Pradesh

29. The President can ask for constitutional advice from which of the following courts?
    (a) Any High Court
    (b) The Supreme Court
    (c) Lok Adalats
    (d) Sessions Court

30. Which of the following Union Territory does not have its own High Court?
    (a) Delhi
    (b) Jammu and Kashmir
    (c) Puducherry
    (d) None of the above

31. Seats are not reserved in Panchayati Raj institutions for which of the following?
    (a) Women   (b) Schedule Castes
    (c) Students   (d) Schedule Tribes

32. The Chairman of Zila Parishad is chosen from ....
    (a) State Administrative Services
    (b) Village Members
    (c) Block development officers
    (d) Ministers of the State

33. The National Food Security Mission for achieving food security was launched in which Five Year Plan?
    (a) Sixth Five Year Plan
    (b) Eleventh Five Year Plan
    (c) Third Five Year Plan
    (d) Fourth Five Year Plan

34. Production of Petroleum in oil refineries is included in which of the following sector of Economy?
    (a) Primary Sector
    (b) Tertiary Sector
    (c) Quaternary Sector
    (d) Secondary Sector

35. The Tendulkar Committee to estimate poverty in India was appointed in ....
    (a) 1991
    (b) 2005
    (c) 2011
    (d) 1951

36. Which of the following measures can help in reducing unemployment in India?
    (a) Starting vocational training institutes
    (b) Expanding MGNREGA Program
    (c) Starting labour intensive industries
    (d) All of the above

37. Which of the following was the first bank note printed in India?
(a) ₹ 20 note   (b) ₹ 500 note
(c) ₹ 1 note   (d) ₹ 10 note

38. Which of the following is the second largest bank of India?
(a) Bank of Baroda
(b) State Bank of India
(c) HDFC Bank
(d) Punjab National Bank

39. Which of the following was the first submarine of India?
(a) INS Kalvari
(b) INS Chakra
(c) INS Arighat
(d) INS Vela

40. Which of the following is not a search engine?
(a) Yahoo   (b) Duck Duck Go
(c) Bing   (d) Ubuntu

2 Marks Questions

41. Match the following.

List I (Sportsperson)		List II (Awards)
A.	Pullela Gopichand	1. Rajiv Gandhi Khel Ratna
B.	Vishwanathan Anand	2. Arjuna Award
C.	Sachin Tendulkar	3. Dronacharya Award
D.	Hima Das	4. Bharat Ratna

Codes

	A	B	C	D		A	B	C	D
(a)	1	4	3	2	(b)	3	2	1	4
(c)	3	1	4	2	(d)	1	3	2	4

42. Which of the following is matched correctly?

	Movement	Leader
1.	Champaran	Rajendra Prasad
2.	Bardoli Satyagraha	Sardar Vallabh Bhai Patel
3.	Quit India Movement	Bhagat Singh

Codes
(a) Only 1 and 2   (b) Only 1 and 3
(c) Only 2 and 3   (d) 1, 2 and 3

43. Find the incorrect pair from the following.

	National Park/Wild Life Sanctuary	State/UT
(a)	Pench National Park	Jharkhand
(b)	Jaldapara Wildlife Sanctuary	West Bengal
(c)	Hemis National Park	Ladakh
(d)	Bandipur Wildlife Sanctuary	Karnataka

44. Find the incorrect pair from the following.

	Famous Personality	Associated with
(a)	Medha Patkar	Narmada Bachao Aandolan
(b)	Verghese Kurien	White Revolution
(c)	Sundar Lal Bahuguna	Chipko Andolan
(d)	M.S. Swaminathan	Metro Rail Transport

45. Consider the following statements about climatic zones of the Earth.

1. The Torrid zone lies between the Tropic of Cancer and Tropic of Capricorn.
2. Polar regions fall under frigid zone and experience the midnight Sun.
3. The Sun is never directly overhead in both the temperate zones.

Which of the following is/are true?

Codes
(a) Only 1 and 2   (b) Only 2 and 3
(c) Only 1 and 3   (d) All of these

46. Match the following.

Famous Site		Located In
A.	Bara Imambara	1. Murshidabad
B.	Buland Darwaza	2. Fatehpur Sikri
C.	Salarjung Museum	3. Lucknow
D.	Hazar Duari Palace	4. Hyderabad

Codes

	A	B	C	D		A	B	C	D
(a)	4	1	2	3	(b)	4	2	1	3
(c)	3	2	4	1	(d)	3	4	2	1

47. Consider the following statements.

1. The Biography of Akbar was written by Abul Fazl.
2. Abul Fazl was among the nine gems in Akbar's court.

Which of the statements given above is/are correct?

Codes
(a) Only 1   (b) Only 2
(c) Both 1 and 2   (d) None of these

48. Arrange the following states in order of onset of South West monsoon.

1. Haryana
2. Kerala
3. Andhra Pradesh
4. Madhya Pradesh

Codes
(a) 1, 2, 4, 3   (b) 2, 3, 4, 1
(c) 3, 2, 1, 4   (d) 4, 2, 1, 3

49. Consider the following statements.

1. India has the fifth largest population in the world.
2. Largest proportion of India's population works in the agriculture sector.
3. Uttar Pradesh has the largest proportion of population in India.

Which of the statements given above is/are correct?

Codes
(a) Only 2 and 3   (b) Only 1 and 2
(c) Only 1 and 3   (d) 1, 2 and 3

50. Consider the following statements.

1. The Parliament of India is organised in two houses.
2. The President is the Chairman of Lok Sabha.
3. The Vice-President is the Chairman of Rajya Sabha.

Which of the statements given above is/are correct?

Codes
(a) 1, 2 and 3   (b) Only 1 and 2
(c) Only 1 and 3   (d) All of these

PRACTICE SET 02

1 Mark Questions

1. The first Buddhist Council was held at which of the following places?
   (a) Rajgriha   (b) Vaishali
   (c) Pataliputra   (d) Kashmir

2. India was divided into how many Mahajanpadas during the Ancient period?
   (a) Fifty   (b) Sixteen
   (c) Four   (d) Nine

3. Jizya, a famous religious tax during Mughal period, was abolished by which of the following Emperors?
   (a) Aurangzeb   (b) Akbar
   (c) Humayun   (d) Jahangir

4. Which of the following laid the first telegraph line in India during British Rule?
   (a) William Bentinck (b) Lord Dalhousie
   (c) Lord Minto   (d) Lord Ripon

5. Which among the following was the leader of 1857 revolt in Assam?
   (a) Khan Bahadur
   (b) Tatya Tope
   (c) Maniram Datta
   (d) Begum Hazrat Mahal

6. The famous Battle of Waterloo was fought between which of the following?
   (a) Germany and Britain
   (b) Germany and USA
   (c) France and Britain
   (d) Russia and France

7. Who was the American President when American Civil war broke out?
   (a) George Washington
   (b) John F. Kennedy
   (c) Abraham Lincoln
   (d) James Buchanan

8. Which of the following parts of the Sun is visible during a Solar Eclipse?
   (a) Chromosphere   (b) Photosphere
   (c) Corona   (d) Core

9. Which of these layers of Earth's interior has the highest density?
   (a) Core   (b) Mantle
   (c) Crust   (d) Asthenosphere

10. Which among the following is the largest tributary of river Brahmaputra?
    (a) Teesta   (b) Subansiri
    (c) Manas   (d) Kameng

11. Which of the following soils is made from sand and silt brought down from lofty Himalayas?
    (a) Black Soil   (b) Red Soil
    (c) Alluvial Soil   (d) Laterite Soil

12. Which among the following is the highest dam of India?
    (a) Bhakra Dam (b) Pong Dam
    (c) Tehri Dam   (d) Sardar Sarovar Dam

13. Singrauli Coalfield is located in which of the following states of India?
    (a) Jharkhand   (b) Madhya Pradesh
    (c) Odisha   (d) West Bengal

14. Which of the following is an onshore petroleum oilfield in India?
    (a) Ravva   (b) Mumbai High
    (c) Bassein   (d) Digboi

15. Which of these states is the second largest producer of Coffee in India?
    (a) Karnataka
    (b) West Bengal
    (c) Andhra Pradesh
    (d) Kerala

16. Which of the following is a Kharif Crop?
    (a) Rice   (b) Maize
    (c) Soyabean   (d) All of these

17. The largest number of Jute textile industrial units are located in which of the following states?
    (a) Madhya Pradesh
    (b) West Bengal
    (c) Assam
    (d) Uttar Pradesh

18. The first Aluminium plant of India was established at which of the following places?
    (a) Hirakud   (b) Raniganj
    (c) Kanpur   (d) Hyderabad

19. Which of the following is the longest mountain railway line?
    (a) Kalka Shimla Railway
    (b) Nilgiri Mountain Railway
    (c) Darjeeling Himalayan Railway
    (d) Matheran Hill Railway

20. The National Waterway II is located in which of the following states?
    (a) Meghalaya   (b) Assam
    (c) Kerala   (d) Uttar Pradesh

21. Which of the following South Indian languages is spoken by largest number of people?
    (a) Telugu   (b) Tamil
    (c) Kannada   (d) Malayalam

22. Mount Harriet National Park is located in which of the following Territories of India?
    (a) Lakshadweep Island
    (b) Madhya Pradesh
    (c) Arunachal Pradesh
    (d) Andaman and Nicobar Island

23. Which of the following is the largest ecosystem on Earth?
    (a) Sahara Desert
    (b) World Oceans
    (c) Amazon Rainforest
    (d) Grasslands

24. The Constituent Assembly adopted the National Anthem of India in which of the following years?
    (a) 1947   (b) 1948   (c) 1949   (d) 1950

25. Which among the following personalities made a handwritten copy of the Constitution?
    (a) Rammanohar Sinha
    (b) Nandlal Bose
    (c) Dr. B.R Ambedkar
    (d) Prem Bihari Narain

26. Which of the following Fundamental Rights cannot be suspended even during an emergency?
    (a) Right to Equality
    (b) Right against Exploitation
    (c) Right to Life
    (d) Cultural and Educational Rights

27 Which of the following is a Socialist Directive Principle of State Policy?
(a) To organise village panchayats
(b) To secure equal pay for equal work
(c) To protect historical monuments
(d) To secure Uniform Civil Code

28. Which among the following was appointed as the Acting Prime Minister after the death of Jawahar Lal Nehru?
(a) Indira Gandhi
(b) Rajiv Gandhi
(c) Lal Bahadur Shastri
(d) Gulzari Lal Nanda

29. Who among the following is usually chosen as the Chief Justice of the Supreme Court?
(a) The Seniormost Judge
(b) The Judge recommended by the President
(c) The Judge who is near his retirement age
(d) None of the above

30. The district court can solve which of the following cases?
(a) Civil matters
(b) Constitutional matters
(c) Criminal matters
(d) Both (a) and (c)

31. Panchayati Raj institutions are mentioned in which of the following sections of the Constitution?
(a) Fundamental Rights
(b) Directive Principles of State Policy
(c) Fundamental Duties
(d) None of the above

32. Which of the following Schedules contain the powers of Panchayats?
(a) Third Schedule   (b) Fifth Schedule
(c) Eleventh Schedule (d) Tenth Schedule

33. Which Five Year Plan of India launched by Indira Gandhi focussed on elimination of Poverty?
(a) First FYP   (b) Third FYP
(c) Fourth FYP   (d) Fifth FYP

34. Banking and financial services are included in which of the following sectors of Indian Economy?
(a) Primary Sector (b) Secondary Sector
(c) Tertiary Sector (d) Quarternary Sector

35. Disguised unemployment in India can be directly reduced by which of the following measures?
(a) Development of Agriculture
(b) Opening of Schools
(c) Universal Basic Income
(d) Opening Jan Dhan Accounts

36. C. Rangarajan Committee to measure poverty in India was setup in which of the following years.
(a) 2011   (b) 1911   (c) 2014   (d) 1978

37. The Indian rupee note does not have denomination in which of the following languages?
(a) English   (b) Urdu
(c) Kashmiri   (d) Bodo

38. Which of the following banks in India work on mainly digital platforms?
(a) Public Commercial Banks
(b) Private Sector Banks
(c) Payments Banks
(d) Cooperative Banks

39. Which of the following is a Battle tank of India?
(a) Mirage
(b) Marut
(c) Rudra
(d) Bhishma

40. Chandrayan II will explore which of the following regions of moon?
(a) North Pole
(b) South Pole
(c) Metius Crater
(d) Dark side of Moon

2 Marks Questions

41. Which of the following is matched correctly?

	Hill Station	Mountain Range
1.	Ooty	Nilgiri Hills
2.	Manali	Himalayas
3.	Mount Abu	Aravallis

Codes
(a) Only 1
(b) Only 2 and 3
(c) Only 1 and 3
(d) All of these

42. Which of the following is matched correctly?

	Newspaper during National Movement	Started By
1.	Kesari	Bal Gangadhar Tilak
2.	Young India	Mahatma Gandhi
3.	Bande Matram	Rabindra Nath Tagore

Codes
(a) Only 2 and 3
(b) Only 1 and 3
(c) Only 1 and 2
(d) 1, 2 and 3

43. Match the following.

	Vitamin		Source
A.	Vitamin C	1.	Almonds
B.	Vitamin E	2.	Fish
C.	Vitamin B12	3.	Kiwi Fruit

Codes

	A	B	C
(a)	3	2	1
(b)	3	1	2
(c)	2	1	3
(d)	1	2	3

44. Match the following.

	Dance Form		State
A.	Kuchipudi	1.	Kerala
B.	Kathak	2.	Andhra Pradesh
C.	Kathakali	3.	Uttar Pradesh

Codes

	A	B	C			A	B	C
(a)	3	2	1		(b)	2	3	1
(c)	2	1	3		(d)	3	1	2

45. Consider the following statements.

1. The first Battle of Panipat was won by Babur.
2. The second Battle of Panipat was won by Sher Shah Suri.

Which of the statements given above is/are correct?

Codes
(a) Both 1 and 2
(b) Only 1
(c) Only 2
(d) None of these

46. Consider the following statements.

1. Indian Monsoon season starts in the Month of June.
2. South West Monsoon contributes to the largest share of rainfall in India.
3. States on Eastern Coast are most affected by Cyclones.

Which of the statements given above is/are correct?

Codes
(a) 1, 2 and 3   (b) 2 and 3
(c) 1 and 3   (d) 1 and 2

47. Consider the following statements.

1. The first census of India was conducted after Independence.
2. The UT of Lakshadweep has the smallest population in India.
3. More than half of India's population Is Tribal.

Which of the statements given above is/are correct?

Codes
(a) Only 3   (b) Only 2
(c) Only 1   (d) Only 1 and 2

48. Consider the following statements.

1. The Prime Minister of India can be a member of either Lok Sabha or Rajya sabha
2. The President is the head of the Cabinet
3. The Governor is the chairman of Vidhan Sabha

Which of the statements given above is/are correct?

Codes
(a) Only 1 and 3   (b) Only 1 and 2
(c) Only 1   (d) All of these

49. Match the following.

List I (Sportsperson)	List II (Associated With)
A. Rajyavardhan Singh Rathore	1. Football
B. Baichung Bhutia	2. Hockey
C. Dhanraj Pillay	3. Wrestler
D. Babita Phogat	4. Shooting

Codes

	A	B	C	D			A	B	C	D
(a)	1	3	2	4		(b)	4	1	2	3
(c)	3	4	1	2		(d)	2	3	4	1

50. From the following statements find out which national park is mentioned here.

1. This national park is located in Umaria district of Madhya Pradesh.
2. The park has a high density of tiger population.
3. The park was established in 1968 and a portion formed into tiger reserve in 1993.

Codes
(a) Pench National Park
(b) Bandhavgarh National Park
(c) Panna National Park
(d) Kanha National Park

Answers

Chapter 1   Ancient History

1. (d)	**2.** (c)	**3.** (d)	**4.** (a)	**5.** (a)	**6.** (b)	**7.** (d)	**8.** (c)	**9.** (c)	**10.** (d)
11. (a)	**12.** (a)	**13.** (c)	**14.** (b)	**15.** (b)	**16.** (a)	**17.** (d)	**18.** (d)	**19.** (a)	

Chapter 2   Medieval History

1. (b)	**2.** (c)	**3.** (a)	**4.** (c)	**5.** (b)	**6.** (c)	**7.** (a)	**8.** (b)	**9.** (c)	**10.** (b)
11. (b)	**12.** (c)	**13.** (d)	**14.** (d)	**15.** (d)	**16.** (d)	**17.** (c)	**18.** (c)	**19.** (d)	**20.** (b)

Chapter 3   Modern History

1. (b)	**2.** (d)	**3.** (b)	**4.** (c)	**5.** (d)	**6.** (c)	**7.** (c)	**8.** (c)	**9.** (d)	**10.** (c)
11. (b)	**12.** (d)	**13.** (c)	**14.** (d)	**15.** (c)	**16.** (b)	**17.** (b)	**18.** (a)	**19.** (b)	**20.** (d)
21. (c)	**22.** (d)	**23.** (a)							

Chapter 4   National Movement

1. (c)	**2.** (d)	**3.** (b)	**4.** (b)	**5.** (b)	**6.** (a)	**7.** (a)	**8.** (b)	**9.** (d)	**10.** (b)
11. (b)	**12.** (b)	**13.** (a)	**14.** (a)	**15.** (c)	**16.** (d)	**17.** (b)	**18.** (d)	**19.** (d)	**20.** (c)
21. (d)	**22.** (d)	**23.** (b)	**24.** (a)	**25.** (c)					

Chapter 5   World History

1. (a)	**2.** (d)	**3.** (c)	**4.** (b)	**5.** (a)	**6.** (c)	**7.** (c)	**8.** (d)	**9.** (b)	**10.** (c)
11. (d)	**12.** (c)	**13.** (b)	**14.** (c)	**15.** (b)	**16.** (b)	**17.** (d)			

Chapter 6   Art and Culture

1. (b)	**2.** (c)	**3.** (a)	**4.** (d)	**5.** (b)	**6.** (d)	**7.** (d)	**8.** (b)	**9.** (b)	**10.** (b)
11. (c)	**12.** (d)	**13.** (a)	**14.** (b)	**15.** (d)	**16.** (b)				

Chapter 7   Our Universe and Earth

1. (c)	**2.** (a)	**3.** (b)	**4.** (b)	**5.** (d)	**6.** (b)	**7.** (d)	**8.** (c)	**9.** (c)	**10.** (b)
11. (d)	**12.** (b)	**13.** (d)	**14.** (c)	**15.** (b)	**16.** (a)	**17.** (d)	**18.** (b)	**19.** (c)	**20.** (c)
21. (a)	**22.** (d)	**23.** (b)	**24.** (b)	**25.** (d)	**26.** (d)	**27.** (a)	**28.** (a)	**29.** (d)	

Chapter 8   Continents

1. (d)	**2.** (c)	**3.** (a)	**4.** (c)	**5.** (d)	**6.** (c)	**7.** (d)	**8.** (c)	**9.** (d)	**10.** (b)
11. (c)	**12.** (c)	**13.** (d)	**14.** (b)	**15.** (d)	**16.** (a)	**17.** (b)	**18.** (b)	**19.** (c)	**20.** (b)
21. (c)	**22.** (b)	**23.** (c)	**24.** (c)	**25.** (c)	**26.** (b)				

Chapter 9   India : Size, Location and Physical Features

1. (c)	2. (d)	3. (b)	4. (b)	5. (d)	6. (c)	7. (d)	8. (b)	9. (c)	10. (c)
11. (b)	12. (d)	13. (c)	14. (d)	15. (c)	16. (b)	17. (c)	18. (c)	19. (b)	20. (c)
21. (b)	22. (c)	23. (c)	24. (c)	25. (c)	26. (a)	27. (c)	28. (c)	29. (d)	30. (a)
31. (d)									

Chapter 10   India Drainage and Climate

1. (a)	2. (b)	3. (c)	4. (b)	5. (c)	6. (b)	7. (c)	8. (c)	9. (c)	10. (d)
11. (a)	12. (d)	13. (c)	14. (c)	15. (b)	16. (a)	17. (c)	18. (a)		

Chapter 11   India : Land, Soil and Water Resources

1. (b)	2. (b)	3. (b)	4. (b)	5. (c)	6. (c)	7. (d)	8. (b)	9. (b)	10. (b)
11. (c)	12. (b)	13. (c)	14. (c)	15. (b)	16. (d)	17. (a)	18. (c)	19. (d)	20. (d)
21. (b)									

Chapter 12   India : Minerals and Energy Resources

1. (d)	2. (d)	3. (c)	4. (b)	5. (c)	6. (c)	7. (d)	8. (d)	9. (c)	10. (d)
11. (b)	12. (c)	13. (c)	14. (d)	15. (b)	16. (c)	17. (c)	18. (c)	19. (d)	20. (c)
21. (d)									

Chapter 13   India : Agriculture

1. (c)	2. (b)	3. (a)	4. (c)	5. (c)	6. (d)	7. (d)	8. (d)	9. (d)	10. (d)
11. (d)	12. (d)	13. (c)	14. (c)	15. (b)	16. (c)	17. (c)	18. (b)	19. (b)	20. (a)

Chapter 14   India : Industries

1. (c)	2. (c)	3. (a)	4. (b)	5. (c)	6. (a)	7. (c)	8. (b)	9. (d)	10. (b)
11. (c)	12. (c)	13. (b)	14. (b)	15. (c)	16. (b)				

Chapter 15   India : Transport and Communication

1. (b)	2. (d)	3. (d)	4. (c)	5. (b)	6. (b)	7. (b)	8. (a)	9. (d)	10. (c)
11. (d)	12. (b)	13. (c)	14. (c)	15. (c)	16. (c)	17. (d)	18. (c)	19. (d)	

Chapter 16   India : Human Resource (Population)

1. (d)	2. (c)	3. (d)	4. (d)	5. (a)	6. (a)	7. (b)	8. (c)	9. (c)	10. (c)
11. (c)	12. (d)	13. (b)	14. (c)	15. (b)	16. (a)	17. (c)	18. (c)	19. (c)	20. (c)

Chapter 17   Ecology and Environment

1. (a)	**2.** (d)	**3.** (c)	**4.** (d)	**5.** (d)	**6.** (c)	**7.** (d)	**8.** (d)	**9.** (d)	**10.** (b)
11. (c)	**12.** (b)	**13.** (d)	**14.** (d)	**15.** (c)	**16.** (d)	**17.** (b)	**18.** (a)	**19.** (b)	**20.** (d)
21. (d)	**22.** (c)	**23.** (c)	**24.** (d)	**25.** (b)	**26.** (d)				

Chapter 18   Constitution

1. (b)	**2.** (d)	**3.** (b)	**4.** (d)	**5.** (c)	**6.** (b)	**7.** (c)	**8.** (d)	**9.** (b)	**10.** (b)
11. (c)	**12.** (a)	**13.** (d)	**14.** (d)	**15.** (c)	**16.** (c)	**17.** (c)	**18.** (c)	**19.** (d)	**20.** (b)
21. (a)	**22.** (d)	**23.** (d)	**24.** (d)	**25.** (b)	**26.** (d)				

Chapter 19   Fundamental Rights/Duties and DPSPs

1. (b)	**2.** (c)	**3.** (d)	**4.** (d)	**5.** (b)	**6.** (c)	**7.** (c)	**8.** (b)	**9.** (a)	**10.** (d)
11. (d)	**12.** (d)	**13.** (d)	**14.** (b)	**15.** (d)	**16.** (d)	**17.** (b)	**18.** (c)	**19.** (d)	**20.** (d)
21. (d)	**22.** (d)								

Chapter 20   Our Government

1. (b)	**2.** (c)	**3.** (c)	**4.** (d)	**5.** (d)	**6.** (d)	**7.** (c)	**8.** (b)	**9.** (a)	**10.** (d)
11. (b)	**12.** (d)	**13.** (b)	**14.** (c)	**15.** (d)	**16.** (b)	**17.** (c)			

Chapter 21   Judiciary

1. (b)	**2.** (c)	**3.** (b)	**4.** (a)	**5.** (c)	**6.** (a)	**7.** (c)	**8.** (c)	**9.** (a)	**10.** (b)
11. (b)	**12.** (d)	**13.** (a)	**14.** (b)	**15.** (c)	**16.** (d)	**17.** (c)	**18.** (c)		

Chapter 22   Panchayati Raj

1. (c)	**2.** (a)	**3.** (c)	**4.** (b)	**5.** (b)	**6.** (c)	**7.** (c)	**8.** (d)	**9.** (c)	**10.** (c)
11. (c)	**12.** (b)	**13.** (c)							

Chapter 23   Indian Economy

1. (b)	**2.** (c)	**3.** (b)	**4.** (b)	**5.** (b)	**6.** (c)	**7.** (d)	**8.** (b)	**9.** (c)	**10.** (b)
11. (b)	**12.** (d)	**13.** (a)	**14.** (c)	**15.** (c)	**16.** (c)	**17.** (a)	**18.** (d)	**19.** (c)	**20.** (d)
21. (d)	**22.** (c)								

Chapter 24   Poverty and Employment

1. (b)	**2.** (b)	**3.** (b)	**4.** (d)	**5.** (d)	**6.** (c)	**7.** (b)	**8.** (d)	**9.** (a)	**10.** (d)
11. (a)	**12.** (b)	**13.** (d)	**14.** (b)	**15.** (c)	**16.** (c)				

Chapter 25 Money and Banking

1. (b)	2. (c)	3. (c)	4. (b)	5. (a)	6. (b)	7. (c)	8. (b)	9. (a)	10. (a)
11. (b)	12. (a)	13. (b)	14. (a)	15. (d)	16. (c)	17. (d)			

Chapter 26 General Science

1. (c)	2. (c)	3. (b)	4. (c)	5. (b)	6. (b)	7. (c)	8. (c)	9. (b)	10. (b)
11. (a)	12. (b)	13. (d)	14. (c)	15. (b)	16. (c)	17. (d)	18. (c)	19. (c)	20. (c)
21. (d)	22. (d)	23. (b)	24. (b)	25. (a)	26. (d)	27. (b)	28. (b)	29. (d)	30. (b)
31. (c)	32. (d)	33. (b)	34. (b)	35. (a)	36. (a)	37. (b)	38. (a)	39. (d)	40. (b)
41. (b)	42. (d)	43. (d)							

Chapter 27 Science and Technology

1. (b)	2. (d)	3. (c)	4. (c)	5. (b)	6. (c)	7. (a)	8. (c)	9. (b)	10. (b)
11. (b)	12. (d)	13. (b)	14. (d)	15. (b)	16. (a)	17. (b)	18. (b)	19. (c)	20. (c)
21. (d)	22. (b)	23. (d)							

Chapter 28 General Knowledge

1. (a)	2. (b)	3. (c)	4. (c)	5. (c)	6. (c)	7. (c)	8. (a)	9. (c)	10. (c)
11. (c)	12. (b)	13. (c)	14. (b)	15. (b)	16. (b)	17. (b)	18. (b)	19. (b)	20. (c)
21. (b)	22. (b)	23. (b)	24. (c)	25. (a)	26. (a)	27. (a)	28. (b)	29. (c)	30. (d)
31. (a)	32. (d)	33. (c)	34. (b)	35. (d)	36. (c)	37. (a)	38. (b)	39. (c)	40. (b)
41. (a)	42. (b)	43. (c)	44. (d)	45. (b)					

Practice Set 1

1. (c)	2. (c)	3. (b)	4. (b)	5. (b)	6. (c)	7. (b)	8. (b)	9. (b)	10. (d)
11. (b)	12. (c)	13. (c)	14. (b)	15. (d)	16. (c)	17. (b)	18. (c)	19. (b)	20. (b)
21. (c)	22. (c)	23. (c)	24. (a)	25. (b)	26. (d)	27. (b)	28. (d)	29. (b)	30. (c)
31. (c)	32. (a)	33. (b)	34. (d)	35. (b)	36. (d)	37. (c)	38. (d)	39. (a)	40. (d)
41. (c)	42. (a)	43. (a)	44. (d)	45. (d)	46. (c)	47. (c)	48. (b)	49. (a)	50. (c)

Practice Set 2

1. (a)	2. (b)	3. (b)	4. (b)	5. (c)	6. (c)	7. (c)	8. (c)	9. (a)	10. (b)
11. (c)	12. (c)	13. (b)	14. (d)	15. (d)	16. (d)	17. (b)	18. (a)	19. (a)	20. (b)
21. (a)	22. (d)	23. (b)	24. (d)	25. (d)	26. (c)	27. (b)	28. (d)	29. (a)	30. (d)
31. (b)	32. (c)	33. (d)	34. (c)	35. (a)	36. (c)	37. (d)	38. (c)	39. (d)	40. (b)
41. (d)	42. (c)	43. (b)	44. (b)	45. (b)	46. (d)	47. (b)	48. (c)	49. (b)	50. (b)

www.ingramcontent.com/pod-product-compliance
Lightning Source LLC
LaVergne TN
LVHW080724170726
843469LV00082B/1906